PENNY TASSONI

UNDERSTANDING CHILDREN'S BEHAVIOUR

Learning to be with others in the Early Years

FEATHERSTONE

FEATHERSTONE
Bloomsbury Publishing Plc
50 Bedford Square, London, WC1B 3DP, UK

BLOOMSBURY, FEATHERSTONE and the Feather logo are trademarks of Bloomsbury Publishing Plc

First published in Great Britain, 2018 by Bloomsbury Publishing Plc

A catalogue record for this book is available from the British Library

ISBN: PB: 978-1-4729-5267-7; ePDF: 978-1-4729-5268-4; ePub: 978-1-4729-5269-1

2 4 6 8 10 9 7 5 3 1

Text design by Lynda Murray

Printed and bound in India by Replika Press Pvt. Ltd.

FSC www.fsc.org
MIX
Paper from responsible sources
FSC® C016779

All papers used by Bloomsbury Publishing Plc are natural, recyclable products from wood grown in well managed forests. The manufacturing processes conform to the environmental regulations of the country of origin

To find out more about our authors and books visit www.bloomsbury.com and sign up for our newsletters

For my granddaughter, Sofia.

Contents

Learning to be with others

Humans are social beings, yet learning to be with others takes time. Young children begin this journey from birth and through first-hand experiences start to map out a picture of what responses are expected of them and how to respond to others. It is a complex journey because some of the things that children learn are acceptable in one context but not in another. It may be fine to run outdoors, but this may be curtailed indoors. In addition, not all adults respond in the same way and – just to make things particularly difficult – some adults say one thing, yet do another!

Our job working with children is to help them navigate the complexities of social behaviour and to support the development of self-regulation, communication and empathy.

This book is divided into sections:

1. ***Developing a shared understanding***
2. ***Understanding children's behaviour and responses***
3. ***Factors affecting children's behaviour and responses***
4. ***Top tips to create a positive environment***
5. ***Practical ways to support children's behaviour***
6. ***An A–Z of behaviours***

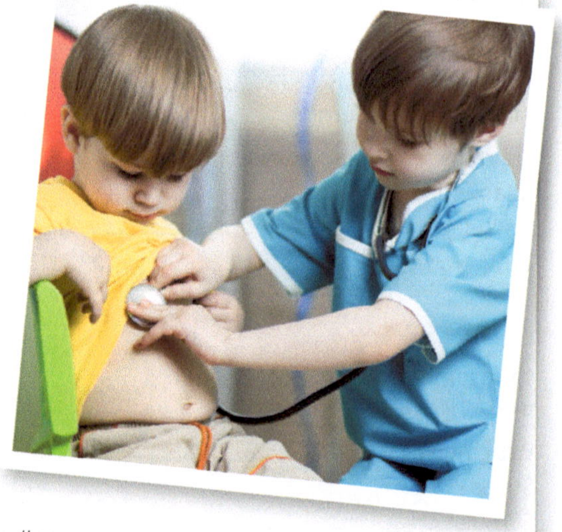

There are many reasons why you may be reading this book. It may be that you have a child whose behaviour is causing you concern or you are developing a behaviour policy for your setting. It may be that you want to learn more about child development or that you wish to improve your skills. Whatever your reasons, I hope that you will find this an interesting book and that it will help you to question and reflect on your practice.

Penny Tassoni

Chapter 1

Developing a shared understanding

It is helpful, if you are working alongside other adults, to come together and develop a shared understanding about the behaviours that you seek to promote in children. No doubt the conversations will turn to your own experiences of childhood and the expectations that adults at the time had. It is worth exploring these further, as some of our beliefs about what is important to foster in children will have been shaped by our own childhoods. It is likely that a range of different viewpoints will emerge and these will need to be explored in order that, eventually, as a team, you are able to come to a shared understanding of what values, behaviours and attitudes you think need to be fostered in the children you work with.

DISCUSSION POINTS

- What were your experiences as a child like? Were you ever physically disciplined, for example?
- If you are a parent, what are you trying to impress upon your own children?
- What strategies do you feel are useful when working with children?
- What boundaries are in place in your setting?
- How are these enforced?

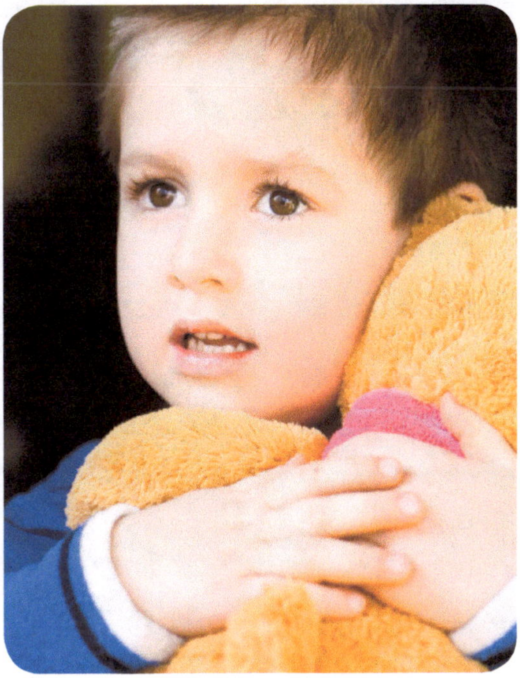

The difference between customs and pro-social behaviours

In your discussions, you may find it helpful to separate out 'customs' or manners from pro-social behaviours.

It is customary for many people in the UK to say 'please' if they want something. Interestingly, this is not a universal custom; other cultures and languages use 'thank you' or the tone of voice instead. Many customs and manners are carried out without much thought as they become habits, but they are important as they are expected by others. It is a custom, for example, not to talk loudly during a film at the cinema or for children not to run around in the library. In your setting, there are also likely to be customs or habits that are linked to health and safety or its smooth running.

Pro-social behaviours are different and are often the common thread between different traditions and cultures. They are acts that involve altruism, care and thought for others. Giving another child a toy when they look upset is an example of pro-social behaviour, as is offering to help someone carry a bag when they are laden. In some ways, it could be argued that developing pro-social behaviours in children needs to be given priority over customs. Children who are cited as being popular by other children tend to exhibit higher levels of pro-social behaviours.

DISCUSSION POINTS

- **Make a list of customs in your setting.**
- **Which customs are linked to culture and tradition?**
- **Are any customs linked to the smooth running of your setting?**

Young children can develop pro-social behaviours

The dangers of a highly authoritarian regime

When discussing behaviour in your setting, watch out for suggestions that children should simply 'do as they are told' without discussion or to please an adult. This was a traditional way in which children used to be expected to behave. Blind obedience is not, in my view, what we need to encourage in young children. While it was (and still is, in some cultures) the expectation of how children needed to behave, it is at best unhelpful and at worst dangerous for a child. Children who only do things to avoid being reprimanded are likely to show very different behaviour when left to their own devices. Harsh discipline is also associated with higher levels of aggression and lower levels of empathy. In addition, it leaves children more vulnerable to abusive adults as children may have learnt that you always have to do what an adult wants.

DISCUSSION POINTS

- **Do you or other adults in your setting often finish sentences with 'for me'? For example, 'can you pick that up for me?' or 'are you going to be good for me, today?'.**
- **How do you ensure that children are learning about *why* rules or expectations are in place in your setting?**

What does it mean to be child centred?

Traditionally, children were reared to 'be seen and not heard'. Today, this harsh approach is not appropriate. Instead, adults are encouraged to be child centred. This term is worth unpicking, especially if you work in a team. Does child centred mean that children can do what they want? Does it mean that children must not be reprimanded? Does it mean that children make the key decisions?

Personally, I take the term 'child centred' to mean that the adults' role is to be very aware of children's needs and to meet them. It means being empathetic to children when they are distressed or facing disappointment, while also helping children to fulfil their potential. I believe that it also means that adults create and take opportunities to ensure that children develop emotional and social skills. This will, at times, mean that they may have to learn to wait or may not be able to have everything they want or see; this is an important part of learning to self-regulate (see page 23). But it also means that children will need (according to their age and stage of development) to be consulted and given some opportunities to learn about decision making and its consequences.

The trick is to make sure that children are given age and stage appropriate decisions and opportunities to be empowered and to develop confidence in their own abilities. This might mean that babies are encouraged to wipe their own faces at mealtimes and that three-year-olds choose which game to play or whether to be indoors or outdoors.

Sadly, there has been a well-meaning trend for some parents to give their children a lot of responsibility at a very young age when children, because of their age and experience, are unable to make informed choices. It is not child centred to give a young child a choice of whether or not they have a vaccination, for example, because the child simply does not have sufficient knowledge or cognitive ability to understand the long-term consequences of the decision they are making. Interestingly, when children are given inappropriate responsibility and lack of opportunities to develop self-regulation, they are more likely to have emotional and behavioural difficulties. It would appear that some children can become anxious in these situations, as being in charge of adults is quite stressful. This often surprises parents who may have made a decision to be child centred because they wanted their child to be confident. Other children find it hard to self-regulate because they have not had any curbs put on their behaviour. This can make it harder for children to make friends and to cope with the demands of being in a group setting where some level of cooperativeness is required.

DISCUSSION POINTS

- **What do you feel is a 'child centred' approach when it comes to helping children develop social and emotional skills?**
- **Give examples of how, in practice, children can be given responsibility and learn to make decisions.**

Developing a behaviour policy

A behaviour policy is in some ways a mission statement. It should explain what your goals are for children in your setting. It should explain how your ways of working will support children, as well as set out the strategies that adults should use when children are showing unwanted behaviour. I also think that a behaviour policy should outline expected behaviour and responses of adults towards children.

As well as being a guide for adults in the setting, it is also important that parents understand the aims of your behaviour policy. This is particularly important as it may be that parents have a very different philosophy of how children should be raised. If the differences are irreconcilable, it is better for everyone to know this at the start!

DISCUSSION POINTS

- **When was the last time that your behaviour policy was reviewed?**
- **Does it accurately reflect your current thoughts and ideas about supporting children's social and emotional development?**
- **How do you share its practical implications with other adults, including staff?**

Working with parents

Parents play an essential role in the development of children's social skills. They influence children's views of others and reinforce customs, attitudes and behaviours. This means that creating a partnership with parents is important. In the same way that all children are unique, so too are all parents. Every parent's circumstances will be different, as will their parenting style and beliefs about social behaviour. While some parents will be very relaxed and rarely curtail their child's activities, others may be very proactive to the point of being aggressively authoritarian in style.

While the ideal is that there is consistency between setting and home, the reality is that there will always be some differences. While some of these will be linked to how parents interact with their children, others will occur because of the different nature of the environments, e.g. a child at home may be allowed to wander freely into the kitchen, but not necessarily in an early years setting.

The emotional bond between parent and child is unique

There are also likely to be other differences because of the intense emotions that parents have towards their children. Parents are likely at times to feel pride, anger and guilt, as well as sheer joy. While practitioners may also feel these emotions towards the children that they work with, they are unlikely to be as intense. This allows us to moderate our responses which in some situations can be beneficial. Having said this, the intense emotion that parents feel is essential to their ability to parent and allows them to perceive their children in a unique way.

Talking through the behaviour policy

It is often useful to have a discussion about how your setting supports children's behaviour before there is a problem. The behaviour policy is a good starting point as it should outline the goals in terms of behaviour as well as how you intend to keep children safe and help them to learn social skills in your setting. When talking about behaviour, it is helpful to find out what things are important to parents and the strategies that they use at home.

For some parents, the general direction taken at home will be fairly similar to your aims in the setting. On the other hand, this type of discussion may reveal that you have very different approaches and even views about children. If this is the case, it is worth finding a compromise which might be along the lines of 'my turf, my rules'. On a related note, it is also worth agreeing with parents what should happen if the child's behaviour needs curbing when you are both present, e.g. at the end of the session. This is important because when children sense that adults are unsure, they may feel the need to explore what the boundaries are. Agreeing who should take over at what point can therefore help children feel more secure when a transition is taking place.

Sharing information with parents

One of the sometimes difficult decisions to make is what and when to share information relating to a child's behaviour with parents. While some parents will take the view that unless very serious, they will leave a setting to sort things out, other parents prefer to know exactly what their child has been doing. In the latter group, some parents will also feel the need to reprimand or punish the child again, and this may backfire in terms of a child's overall development. There is also a danger to only share information that relates to 'problems' as opposed to celebrating moments of self-regulation or pro-social behaviours. Celebrating when children show these is important because it helps to value these skills.

When it comes to sharing information with parents, it can be worth developing a set of guidelines, as part of your behaviour policy, as to when and what will be shared. This is an area for a team discussion, but my personal take is that, by and large, incidents that are developmentally typical and have had little impact on the child or on other children should not be raised routinely with parents. The exception would be in cases where the behaviour is very unusual for the child or where patterns of behaviour are developing, e.g. a child keeps snatching things or has several tantrums in the course of a session. In such cases, it is helpful to talk to parents and to see if together you can work out what might be the cause as well as agreeing a consistent approach.

While low-level behaviours that are developmentally typical may not be routinely reported, behaviours where other children are hurt, such as biting, do need to be shared with parents, as do behaviours that are atypical. It is not that parents will be able to influence these behaviours from afar (children are not on remote control), but more because such behaviours may require a joint approach. In the case of atypical behaviours, it is likely to be an indication that children have other needs.

The style in which we talk to parents needs to be sensitive. This is because if parents feel that we are critical of them or their child, they are likely to feel defensive and all hopes of identifying causes and strategies may be lost. However we choose to start a conversation with parents, it is important that we do so out of earshot of the child as well as other children and parents. It is also essential to steer away from an accusatory style – our tone should be reassuring. The reality is that even behaviours that are atypical are not predictive of children's later life chances. The four-year-old who bites out of frustration is unlikely, as a result of that behaviour, to become a hardened criminal. Working together to consider factors that might be influencing a child's response and coming up with a common approach can be beneficial.

DISCUSSION POINTS

- **Do you talk through with parents their aims and strategies in relation to behaviour at home?**
- **In your behaviour policy, do you have guidelines about how, when and what information is shared with parents?**
- **Do you ever get feedback from parents to find out how well they feel that you share information?**
- **As part of staff development, do you role play breaking potentially difficult or awkward news to parents?**

Chapter 2

Understanding children's behaviour and responses

How children learn to respond towards others and also to respond to different situations is very complex. There are many different theories of how children learn behaviour, but no single theory provides a comprehensive explanation. It is likely that different aspects come together like a jigsaw puzzle. Understanding the myriad of ways in which children learn about behaviour may provide some clues as to how to encourage social behaviours. It can also throw light on why some children adopt behaviours and responses that are less welcome. In this section, I outline some of the theories and approaches that might be useful in your day-to-day practice with children.

Operant conditioning

A good starting point for understanding some aspects of how children learn behaviour is to look at operant conditioning. Many techniques employed to modify children's behaviour use Skinner's theory of operant conditioning as their basis. Operant conditioning as a technique has its critics and its limitations – it is worth being aware of these. Most of the original research that supports the theory was carried out on mice and pigeons. These animals do not have the same capabilities to reflect, think and feel emotions in the way that humans do. Operant conditioning does not consider the more complex emotions and internal motivations that may affect our behaviour.

Interestingly, the principles of operant conditioning seem to work more effectively with young children, perhaps because the complexities of thinking and reasoning are not yet fully developed at this age. Having said this, the theories of operant conditioning are used by businesses to encourage adults to spend money with them. In terms of early childhood, it provides a useful explanation of how children learn simple habits – some of which we will want to encourage (such as tidying away toys) and others that will need modifying (such as shouting across a room to get someone's attention). As such, knowing the principles of operant conditioning can be very helpful.

An adult's attention is a powerful positive reinforcer

The idea behind Skinner's theory is that we learn behaviour through our actions and then draw conclusions based on the consequences. Instead of 'consequences', the term 'reinforcers' or 'reinforcements' is used.

Reinforcers are divided into three groups:

1. **positive reinforcers**
2. **negative reinforcers**
3. **punishments**

Positive reinforcers are likely to make us repeat behaviour when something pleasurable occurs or when a need is met in some way as a result of the behaviour. A child who needs attention may tap the back of an adult. If the adult turns around to talk to the child, it is likely that the child will repeat this behaviour in the future. In the same way, if you are given a free sample of cheese in a supermarket, you may be more inclined to buy a packet of it if you liked the taste.

Negative reinforcers are likely to make us repeat behaviour as well, but this is in order to stop something from happening to us – for example, you may change the battery in the smoke detector when it starts to randomly beep in order to put a stop to the noise.

Punishments are likely to stop us from repeating behaviour – for example, we may learn not to touch a hot iron after being burnt.

Positive reinforcers are the way forward

In terms of encouraging children's behaviour, it would appear that children are far more likely to repeat behaviours over a longer term if they have experienced a positive reinforcement. Research shows that negative reinforcements and punishments may stop the behaviour at the time, but in the long run, they are not effective. This is one reason why most settings are encouraged to take a positive rather than a punitive approach with children.

Examples of powerful positive reinforcers

It is worth being aware of some positive reinforcers that seem to be very powerful for most young children. These positive reinforcers often drive some behaviours, both positive and unwanted.

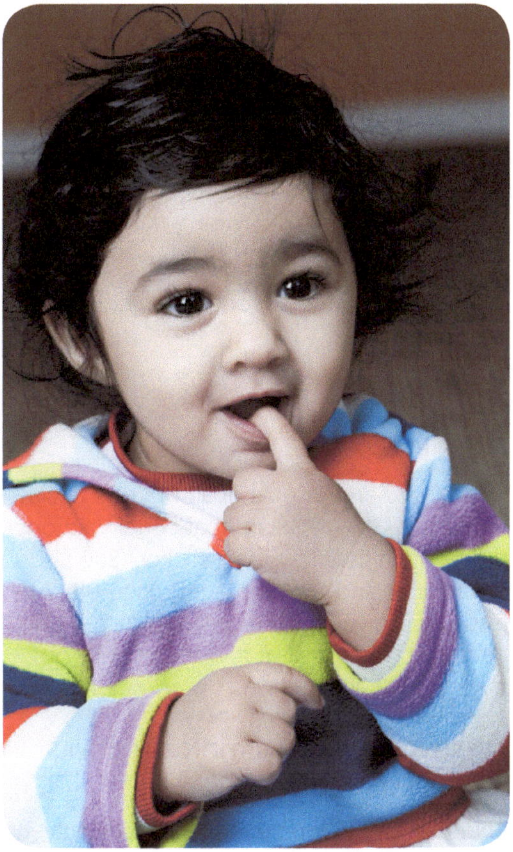

ADULT ATTENTION

For many young children, gaining an adult's attention is a powerful reinforcer. This includes eye contact, conversation or physical acknowledgement such as a cuddle. Adult attention is also given to children when adults praise them or show any form of approval.

Some behaviours that are challenging for adults are equally driven by the need for attention. A common mistake is to assume that reprimanding a child will be a disincentive. This is rarely the case. Reprimanding children whose ambition was to gain attention will usually backfire as, during the reprimand, the child is gaining attention.

Case study

Jamal is two years old. He has been happily playing near his key person, Kat, with some bricks. She has turned to one side to share a story with another child. Jamal plays for a moment, but then picks up a brick and throws it at her back. Kat turns around and tells him to stop and continues sharing the story with the other child. Jamal throws one brick and another in quick succession aiming for her back. Kat turns around and tells Jamal to stop once more. When he throws another brick, she tells him that he will hurt her and then picks up the bricks and tidies them away.

At two years old, Jamal is unlikely to be talking fluently. He cannot explain that he wants her to continue playing or that he is jealous that she is with another child. The first brick was probably an experiment, but by turning around immediately, Kat has positively reinforced the action. Jamal therefore learnt that throwing a brick at her gains her attention.

CHECKPOINTS

- How and when do children gain adult attention in your setting?
- Have any children learnt to gain adult attention by doing things that are not appropriate?
- How do you respond when children do this?

STICKERS

Stickers are an example of a concrete positive reinforcer. Children learn that certain actions will result in their gaining a sticker. (See also advantages and disadvantages, page 68.) As a sticker is given by an adult, the child is also gaining further positive reinforcement from having adult attention.

APPROVAL AND ADMIRATION OF OTHERS

As children become older, how their peers react to them becomes increasingly important. Some children may repeat behaviours that have gained favourable responses from other children, e.g. a child might stick their tongue out and make other children laugh.

SENSORY POSITIVE REINFORCERS

These are positive reinforcers that give children a 'feel-good factor'. It might be that the action of jumping on a sofa feels good and so a child is likely to repeat it. There is a wide range of sensory reinforcements and these include sand, water as well as food or simply going fast on a tricycle. Sensory reinforcers tend to be extremely powerful. Many practitioners will find that once a toddler has discovered an action, such as pushing another child over, they are likely to repeat it even if they have been reprimanded.

Case study

Ayesha is three years old. Today her feet touched the ground as her father was pushing her in the pushchair giving her a strong sensation. Her father told her to stop doing it as she was spoiling her shoes. She put her feet up on the foot bar, but shortly afterwards when she saw that her father was not looking, let her feet fall to the ground.

Ayesha has discovered a new sensation that is pleasing. She repeats the action because she has been positively reinforced by the sensation. She is not trying to gain her father's attention. Every time she is in the pushchair, she is likely to try and repeat this action.

UNEXPECTED POSITIVE REINFORCERS!

While I have provided some examples of positive reinforcers, the reality is that you may not always be able to predict what is going to act as a positive reinforcer. It is only after children have repeated a behaviour that you might start to recognise the reinforcer. A child who has pushed over another child outdoors and was ordered inside might actually prefer to be indoors and so may in future repeat the behaviour as a way of getting sent inside!

Primary and secondary positive reinforcers

Most reinforcers that we use with young children are primary reinforcers. Primary reinforcers are those that once given or found, immediately meet the needs or give pleasure. Chocolate is an example of primary reinforcer – most people find that once they put it into their mouths, they enjoy the taste. As children get older, it is likely that settings will start to use some secondary reinforcers. It is important to understand how secondary reinforcers work. Secondary reinforcers are different because they themselves do not give us satisfaction, but we learn that they symbolise getting primary reinforcement. A good example of secondary reinforcement in our daily lives is money. Coins and notes do not give us rewards, but we learn that they can be used to buy things that will give us primary reinforcement, e.g. a trip to the cinema. Common secondary reinforcers that are used with older children include star charts and also marbles in the jar. (See pages 62-3 for the advantages and disadvantages of star charts.)

Primary reinforcers tend to work better with young children

Time matters

The amount of time between an action or behaviour taking place and the reinforcement seems to matter. Immediate reinforcement is more powerful than delayed reinforcement. A child who is given praise for persevering at a jigsaw puzzle at the time will, in theory, be more affected by this than being praised an hour later. It is thought that the power of immediate reinforcements occurs because the child can make the link between the action and the reinforcement. If you look back at the case studies on pages 13 and 14, you will see that in each case the child experienced immediate reinforcement after the behaviour.

WHY DELAYING A REINFORCEMENT MIGHT BE HELPFUL

There may be times when you need to respond to a child, but choose to delay your response so that the positive reinforcement is not as strong. An example of this might be when a child hurts another child. Rather than reprimanding the child immediately, you may wait and instead focus on the victim. Delaying talking to the child means that they do not gain immediate adult attention from hitting other children.

CHECKPOINTS

- Can you identify a positive reinforcement for a behaviour that a child repeatedly shows?
- What is the timing between the action and the reinforcement?

IN PRACTICE

We have seen that reinforcement seems more powerful if it is given at the time. This has implications for when we praise children or give them a sticker. Ideally, if we wish to promote a positive behaviour, it is worth praising at the time so that the link between action and positive reinforcement is clear. On the other hand, finding a way of delaying reinforcement can be useful if behaviour needs to be changed.

WHAT HAPPENS IF NO REINFORCEMENTS OCCUR?

Practitioners and parents are often told that some behaviours need to be ignored. This can seem puzzling, but is quite an effective strategy especially where the behaviours are driven by the need for adult attention. When an action is not followed by any reinforcement, over time the behaviour is likely to disappear. This is sometimes referred to as 'extinction'. For example, if a child continually taps you on the arm while you are talking to another child and you ignore the behaviour, the child (in theory) should give up this action.

CHECKPOINTS

- Have you ever consistently ignored a child's behaviour when it first occurred?
- Was this difficult to do?

IN PRACTICE

Not reacting to a child's behaviour is very difficult, but can be highly effective as a strategy – especially at the point at which the behaviour occurs. It can also be worth doing something as a distraction, such as getting another toy out, as this can take the focus off the behaviour.

Intermittent reinforcements

As well as ignoring some behaviours, parents and practitioners are often told that they need to be very consistent if they wish to either promote or prevent a behaviour. This piece of advice is valid, and it is linked closely to intermittent reinforcement. Intermittent reinforcement occurs when sometimes a positive reinforcement occurs during or after a behaviour, but not at other times. It would be a little like pressing a faulty light switch – sometimes the light comes on, but sometimes it doesn't.

It would appear that intermittent reinforcement is highly effective and can shape behaviour over the long term. This is great news if the behaviour that is being shown is one that is desirable, but not so good where the behaviour is not wanted.

Case study

Jamie's parents have complained that going shopping with him is a nightmare. In the supermarket, there is a ride; children can sit in the car and music plays if a coin is put in. Jamie's grandmother thought it would be nice for him to try it. Jamie loved it. On the next visit to the supermarket, Jamie spotted the machine and asked to have a go in it. His parents said no. Jamie began to have a tantrum. Jamie's mum eventually managed to get him out of the store. On the next visit, he asked for a ride on the machine. At first the parents said no, but when he started to whine, fearing a tantrum, they let him have a ride. The next time, the parents said no despite Jamie's whining and tantrum. Over the next couple of visits, they maintained this position even though Jamie whined for quite long periods. On his birthday, Jamie pointed at the machine and began to whine. His parents decided that as a treat he could have a go.

Jamie enjoyed the sensation of the moving car along with the music. This was a powerful sensory reinforcer. Jamie has also learned over time that if he whines, sometimes he may get a ride. Each time he has a ride, he is gaining a positive reinforcement and so the whining behaviour is likely to persist for quite a while.

LONG GAPS BETWEEN POSITIVE REINFORCEMENTS

Interestingly, it would appear if there is a run of not getting a positive reinforcement followed by a positive reinforcement, the behaviour becomes stronger. It would seem that the learning that takes place is that persistence eventually pays off. If we put this in an adult context, this is often how some computer games work. It is unlikely that you win every time, but you keep on trying and will eventually be rewarded with a win. The one win after maybe ten tries will be enough to motivate a further few games.

IN PRACTICE

There are a few practical points to pull out about how intermittent reinforcement works. Firstly, in terms of changing a child's behaviour, it is worth considering whether intermittent reinforcement is part of the problem. If so, it will be essential to choose a time when all adults feel that they can be consistent as it may require several days before the behaviour eventually ceases. If the timing is not quite right to tackle the behaviour, ironically, it can be better just to let the child do the behaviour rather than to maintain the inconsistent approach. This is because the research suggests that if a behaviour consistently gains a positive reinforcement and then suddenly the reinforcement ceases, the behaviour is dropped more quickly.

While we have focused on behaviour that needs to be changed, intermittent reinforcement may also be worth thinking about in relation to promoting positive behaviour. It may be that while praising a child may act as a positive reinforcement, it may not be necessary to praise the action every time. This links to what some parents say about their teenagers. If they pay their children for each chore done, the teenagers tend not to do anything just to help out. If, on the other hand, parents give money in a more random way, the teenagers seem to be more likely to help out.

Adults and negative reinforcers

While we have looked at how children may learn behaviours because of reinforcements, we need to be aware that this is not one sided. Adults, too, can get into habits of responding to children. This is often as a result of negative reinforcement. In the case study (page 17), the adult 'gives in' to the child to stop the child from whining or having a tantrum. This is a negative reinforcement as the adult has learnt that to stop the noise, a ride on the machine will work.

Social learning theories

One of the ways that children learn is by watching and listening to adults and other children. They notice how adults respond to other people. They may pick up on what generates laughter, irritation and anger. Over a number of years, there has been significant research looking at this aspect of learning. Albert Bandura has been particularly associated with what was first called 'observational learning' but is now referred to as 'social cognitive theory' or 'social learning theory'. In addition, some neuroscience research has suggested that there are 'mirror neurons' and that our brains are primed to notice and copy what others do.

If you have worked with children for a number of years, you may well have seen how, at times, children seem to copy others. Once a toddler starts banging on a table, others may follow. A child new to the setting may quickly learn to put on a painting apron without anything being said.

The theories of social learning are very interesting and a couple of points from Bandura's work are worth pulling out.

This child is imitating what she has seen an adult do

Conditions for social learning

Adults are often puzzled that children pick up some behaviours and actions, but not others. Bandura suggests that there are four conditions that have to be in place in order for a child to learn from what they have seen:

1. **To begin with, children have to have noticed what is happening and have focused their attention on the event.**

2. **They also have to remember what they have seen. Both concentration and memory are cognitive processes.**

3. **Children also need to be able to repeat the action or behaviour. This may require the resources and/or physical skills.**

4. **Finally, the action or behaviour needs, in some way, to be sufficiently interesting to motivate the child to try it.**

How social learning and operant conditioning often work together

I started this chapter by suggesting that explanations of behaviour are complex and often come together. Social learning, alongside positive reinforcement, can be particularly powerful. A child watches another child hanging up their apron and does the same. An adult smiles and says, 'You hung up your apron. That's great!' The original learning took place by watching, but the adult provided positive reinforcement afterwards. It is therefore highly likely that this action will be repeated. In the case study where Ben copies the action of Anna, below, the action was also reinforced because Ben liked the sound and sensation of the spoon hitting the table. Further reinforcement also comes because Anna giggles and pays attention to him.

Case study

Anna and Ben are waiting for their lunch. Anna picks up the spoon and bangs it on the table. She giggles. Ben is watching her. He picks up his spoon and repeats what Anna has done. Ben loves the feeling and the sound of the spoon hitting the table. He also sees that Anna is smiling.

Ben has learnt to hit the table with the spoon by copying Anna. He has the cognitive ability to remember what Anna did. He has the spoon and also the physical skills to repeat what he saw. Finally, he is motivated to repeat the action because he likes the sound, and he sees that Anna is looking at him and giggling.

Developing responses towards others through social learning

As well as children learning physical actions, it is thought that over time children also internalise the attitudes from the key people in their lives as a result of social learning. A child who sees their parents being warm, trusting and generous towards others may later on approach people in a similar way. Whereas children who regularly see their parents showing mistrust and hostility towards strangers may be more inclined to adopt this view of people as a default.

Show, not tell!

One of the interesting aspects of the social learning theory is that it would appear that children are more likely to take notice of what adults (and other children) *do* rather than what is said to them. A good example of this is smoking. While parents who smoke may tell their children that they should not smoke, this seems to have little impact in later life. It would appear that children are far more influenced by how adults behave than by what they say.

IN PRACTICE

There are many things to reflect on from the social learning theory.

This child is learning about turn taking by playing with an adult

Focusing on adult behaviour and responses within the setting

In terms of our practice, social learning means that we need to be aware that children will be picking up cues in how adults respond and act. In particular, we should be aware that how we deal with stressful situations is likely to affect children. Ideally, children need to see adults who can self-regulate their responses. Children who have repeatedly witnessed adults who shout or storm out are more likely to repeat these behaviours later on.

The table below shows some of the very practical ways in which adults may be able to help children to learn skills and social behaviours.

Ways that adults may role model social skills and behaviours

Situation	Adults can help by:
Mealtimes	• modelling a positive approach towards healthy food • sitting to eat and interact with children • noticing when children need help
Communication	• listening to children without interrupting • going over to colleagues and children rather than shouting across the room
Showing respect and concern	• greeting colleagues, children, parents and visitors warmly • being interested in others' ideas and what they say • noticing when children, colleagues and parents need assistance and acting promptly
Environment	• picking up items from the floor and tidying cheerfully
Hygiene and dressing	• washing hands when required • wearing protective clothing for messy activities • putting on appropriate clothing when going outdoors, e.g. with their coat done up
Play	• taking turns when playing games • not taking over play, but asking children before joining in • asking permission before taking resources if they are using them • modelling how to use toys and resources safely.

Encouraging shared moments

There will be times when children want to join in as they see others doing something that is of interest to them. A child may see you tidy away and want to help, or a two-year-old may see another child playing with a ball and want to have a go. If resources or opportunities are not available, young children may then become frustrated. Indeed, this is often the reason behind tantrums and squabbles that break out. It is therefore important to look at how to support shared moments. It might mean providing additional resources or equipment or encouraging a child to join at the point at which they are interested. Asking toddlers and young children to wait often backfires as, when their turn comes, they are not interested – the moment has passed.

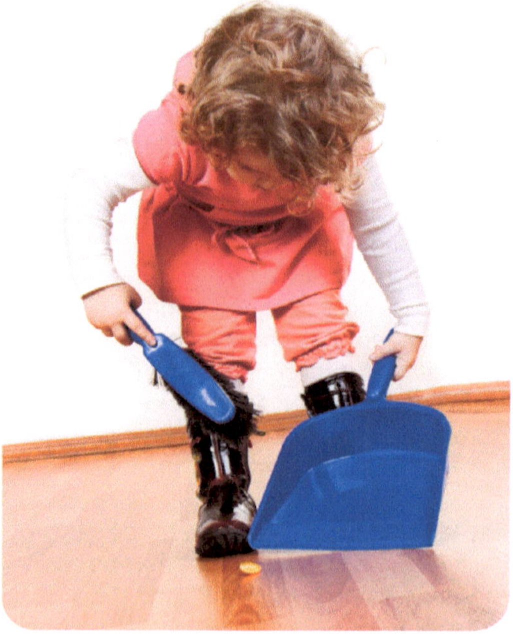

Case study

A preschool has observed that two-year-olds seem to battle over certain pieces of equipment. Trikes and pushchairs seem to be particular objects of squabbles. They have decided to look again at the equipment that is provided outdoors. As an experiment, they removed the trikes and pushchairs and instead created an obstacle course using logs, planks and also a tunnel. One member of the team started to walk on the obstacle course. Quickly a two-year-old started to copy her actions. Shortly afterwards, several other children started to join in.

This preschool has distracted the children by removing the source of conflict. They have provided an opportunity that children can take part in together. By modelling how to use the obstacle course, the adult was able to influence the children's actions. Once more than one child started to use the obstacle course, other children wanted to join. The preschool will need to think about how to re-introduce the wheeled toys in ways that will prevent squabbles. It might be that they simply provide wheeled toys in sufficient quantities to allow many children to use them at once.

Brain maturation and development

In the last few years, there has been increasing interest in how the brain works and develops. The study into this is called neuroscience and, over time, it will no doubt give us more information about the ways in which children learn behaviour. We have known for some time that there is a link between developmental processes and children's ability to show the skills needed for social behaviours. A good example of this is the way that frequent tantrums are common amongst two-year-olds, but occur far less in older groups of children. One of the key things that has emerged from the work of neuroscientists is knowledge about the way in which experiences can change the structures within parts of the brain but also how the brain grows and develops over time. Over the years, a great deal of research has pointed to social skills being linked to development and maturation.

The development of self-regulation

Self-regulation is the ability to control one's impulses. This is needed in order to take turns, but also to prevent us from reacting to strong emotions. In some ways, this is like having a braking system. Everyone reading this must surely have had moments when they have felt like throwing something across a room or saying something rude. If you did not succumb to these impulses, take a while to think about what stopped you. Was it a friend who helped you to calm down, or was it a voice in your head that made you think about the consequences? Self-regulation is linked to children's cognitive and language development. This means that very young children are likely to be impulsive and easily overwhelmed by their emotions. Great strides in self-regulation occur when children start to use language to talk to themselves. This type of language is sometimes called private or inner speech. With toddlers, some of this speech is a repetition of what adults have said to them, e.g. children will point and say 'no' to something that an adult told them not to touch. As children's language develops, so does their ability to self-regulate, although there are other factors at work too. It would appear that children's self-regulation is also linked to their experience of sensitive and consistent care.

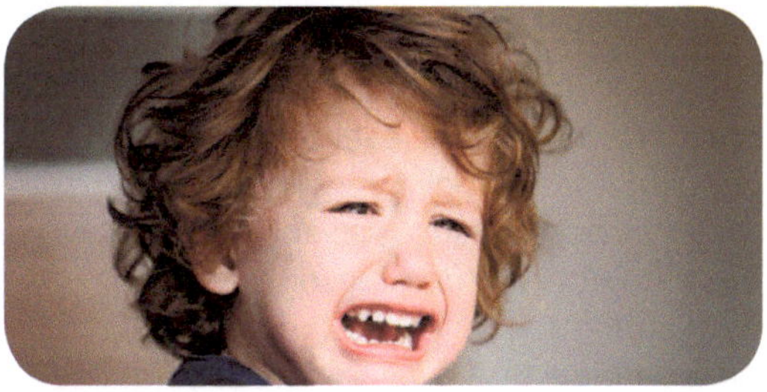

Case study

Zac is fifteen months old. He has learnt that if he is thirsty and points at a beaker, his parent will give him a drink. He has also learnt that he may have to wait a little for it to be filled up, but during this time his parent talks to him.

Zac can recognise the routine of having a drink and knows that his needs are going to be consistently met. Through this process, Zac is learning to control his impulse to have the beaker immediately. He is learning to self-regulate.

IN PRACTICE

While self-regulation is linked to children's development, creating the right environment and opportunities can support children's progress. The following section offers a few practical ways in which we can support children.

PREDICTABILITY

Self-regulation develops more easily in children who have a level of predictability and structure in their lives. This means that they are less stressed and so find it easier to control their feelings. A child who knows that after finishing a meal, the plates are cleared away before the adult is free to play with them, will learn to control their immediate impulses. Consistent adult reactions and routines that are age appropriate also contribute to a sense of predictability.

Case study

Harper lives with two other siblings. Her parent has depression and abuses alcohol and, as a result, is not always able to meet Harper's needs. Harper's home is quite chaotic and untidy. If Harper cries, she is usually ignored or shouted at. At other times, she may be hugged. Her parent is not consistent with expectations. Sometimes the children are threatened with punishment if they make too much noise or jump on and off the sofa; at other times, nothing is said to them. Harper has just started nursery. Harper finds it hard to pay attention or to regulate her emotions.

Harper is having difficulties with self-regulation because her day-to-day experiences have been chaotic. The lack of order and routine means that she cannot predict what is going to happen next. This makes self-regulation harder. The nursery environment may help Harper, if there are predictable routines and her needs are met in a warm and consistent way.

Simple games with adults can help children to develop self-regulation

TURN TAKING

Learning to take turns supports self-regulation. Children need to practise this with adults at first. With toddlers, this might mean rolling a ball back and forth; with older children it might mean an adult holding out a box and two children taking it in turns to put toys back inside to tidy up. As children learn to increasingly self-regulate, the waiting might become longer, e.g. playing a board game with three other children and so having to wait for longer to take a turn.

STEP-BY-STEP

Adults can help children with some activities that require self-regulation by supporting them step by step. This breaks down the activity into manageable components. If a toddler is impatient to play outdoors, the adult might say, 'let's go and get your coat together'. Then, once the coat has been found, the adult – step-by-step – supports the child to get ready. As a result of the adult's support, the child is able to control their impatience and cope with the delay.

The development of theory of mind and empathy

One of the skills needed to be with others is to be able to imagine what they are thinking and their intentions. This is often referred to as 'theory of mind'. The speed at which children develop theory of mind is variable. Toddlers will often start to show some understanding that others have intentions as can be seen by a trick that many children play: the toddler holds out a toy for an adult, but takes it away just as the adult reaches for it. Further development in children's understanding and thinking takes place so that, by the age of four or five, most children can correctly answer this type of scenario correctly: 'A family always keeps biscuits in a biscuit tin. A boy fills that biscuit tin with clothes pegs. What will his mother expect to find when she next opens up the tin?' A child is also likely to be able to explain why the mother would think what she was thinking.

Theory of mind is needed in the development of empathy. Empathy is the ability to feel another person's emotional experience rather than to recognise and sympathise with it in a more general way.

Empathy is a huge motivator in pro-social behaviour, and children who have higher levels of empathy tend to be more popular with other children. Babies are able to detect the difference between a sad face and happy one in the first few months of life and usually at around ten months the difference between a sad voice and a happy one. They reflect these emotions accurately through their own body language. This is sometimes referred to as social referencing. From this point, the ability to recognise emotions continues to develop with older children starting to give simple reasons for another child's sadness or happiness. As well as recognising and experiencing the same or similar emotions, empathy also has a cognitive component. This is the 'action' bit of being empathetic. An adult worried about the plight of a group of refugees may start to collect clothes, for example. The table shows how this develops in four broad stages as proposed by Martin Hoffman.

Stages in the development of empathy[1]

Global empathy	In the first year, a baby will match the strong emotion being shown, e.g. cry if their parent is very upset.
Egocentric empathy	By 18 months, most children will show signs of distress in response to the distress of others. They will act to help the other children, but will do things that they find comforting, e.g. a child may offer their comforter to another child.
Empathy for another's feelings	As early as two years onwards, some children will start to show that they understand and feel the emotions of others. Their actions to comfort others are based more on what the other children might need, e.g. they may get the child's parent or find the child's favourite toy. As children develop further, they are able to respond increasingly to more complex emotions shown by others, e.g. disappointment or jealousy.
Empathy for another's life condition	From adolescence onwards, young people and adults become aware that others' feelings may be linked to more complex life events such as poverty or bereavement. They start also to be empathetic to whole groups of people such as refugees or the homeless.

1. Adapted from Hoffman, M.L. (2001). 'A comprehensive theory of prosocial moral development' in D. Stipek & A. Bohart (EDs.), *Constructive and destructive behavior.* (pp. 61-86). Washington, D.C.: American Psychological Association.

IN PRACTICE

The development of empathy can vary between children. The research shows that there may be a genetic factor involved but the environment that children are in seems to be more important. Before children can show concern and care for others, they need to have experienced being loved and cared for themselves. This is why attachment and the key person system (see page 30) are so important.

- **Recognising and labelling emotions**

To help children understand emotions in others, research would suggest that children whose parents talked about emotions and labelled emotions as they arose were more sensitive to others' emotions. While the research looked at this in relation to parents rather than practitioners, it is likely that this remains an important strategy to use in early years settings.

- **Role modelling**

One of the ways in which we can help young children show care and concern is through role modelling. This means making sure that we show concern and warmth towards children in our day-to-day work even when we are feeling frustrated or irritated.

- **Window into our mind**

As well as role modelling, it is also important that children start to understand what we are thinking in relation to others. This may mean making comments such as 'I think I will sit with Kamal as he looks a little sad'.

- **Recognising children's care and concern for others**

Even babies and toddlers can show concern when other children look upset. Older children may also want to hug or give another child a toy if they are unhappy. These acts often occur spontaneously, but it is important that they are recognised. While praise is probably not the right route, showing some recognition and approval is useful. This might mean saying something such as 'that was a kind thing to do. I am sure Kamal feels better now'.

As children become older, they start to know what others might be thinking

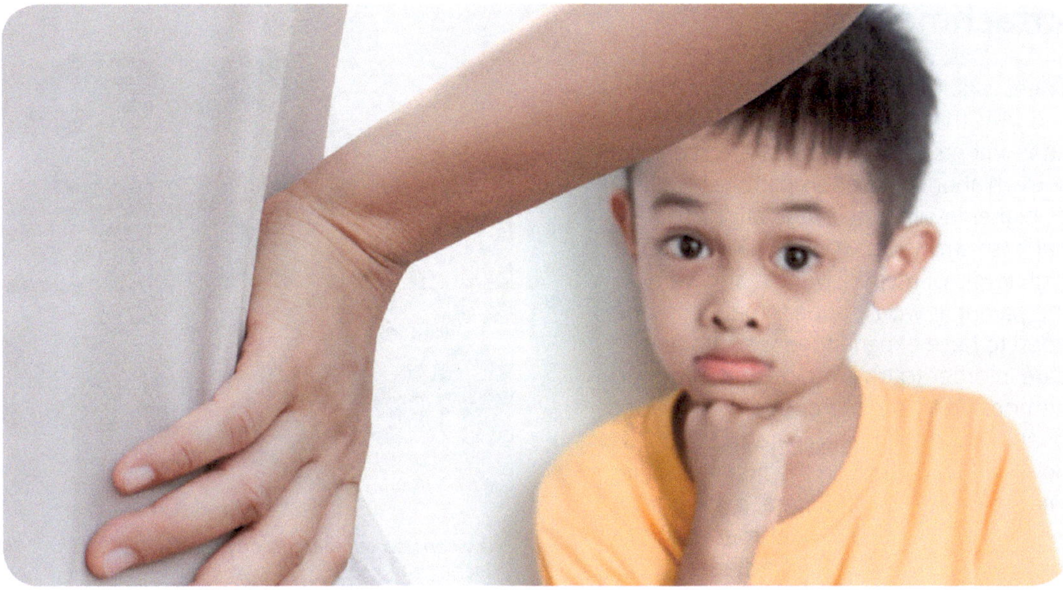

The development of moral reasoning

Knowing 'right' from 'wrong' and acting accordingly is the basis of moral reasoning. It has been the basis of some research and, as with other aspects of development, it looks as if there are clear patterns to how it develops in children. Overall, researchers suggest that very young children are pretty much amoral. They do not have their own morals as such, instead they take their cues about right and wrong from how adults react to them. Feelings of guilt or shame are thought to be more linked to getting caught and responding to adults' disappointment than prompted by guilt about the act. Even as children grow, their decisions about whether to cheat or steal may still be based on whether they will get caught rather than about whether they are likely to feel bad afterwards. The most influential researcher into moral reasoning, Lawrence Kohlberg, suggests that moral reasoning does not fully emerge until adolescence and adulthood.

IN PRACTICE

If we accept that young children are neutral when it comes to morality and learn about right and wrong from adult's reactions, we might need to focus on our own responses. Children will notice what we react to and the strength of our reactions.

This links back to the social learning theory where children pull out meaning from what adults do. It also links to operant conditioning: if children are praised or gain acknowledgement for not cheating or taking things without asking, in theory, they will learn that these are valued responses. Interestingly, there is some research that shows that where adults respond by punishing children, child may simply learn strategies so that they do not get caught.

Children will also need to hear how adults reason when making their decisions, e.g. an adult finds an earring on the floor and says, 'This is pretty! I like it, but I will give it back because it belongs to Annie. She will feel sad if she does not have it back.'

Attachment theory

There is quite a lot of research which suggests that children who have strong attachments to their parents are likely to show higher levels of empathy as well as higher levels of self-regulation. This is because strong attachment is linked to high levels of responsiveness shown by the parent. It would appear that children need to have experienced warmth and care in order to trust others and in turn to demonstrate care and concern. The bond or attachment between parent and child develops particularly in the first year of life. There seems to be a general pattern to the way children develop attachments and the table below summarises the stages.

How can you tell that this child and adult have an attachment?

Stages of attachment

Age	Stage	Features
6 weeks–3 months	Indiscriminate attachments	Babies begin to be attracted to human faces and voices. First smiles begin at around six weeks.
3 months–7/8 months	Indiscriminate attachments	Babies are learning to distinguish between faces showing obvious pleasure when they recognise familiar faces. They are happy to be handled by strangers, preferring to be in human company rather than left alone – hence the term indiscriminate attachments.
Around 7/8 months	Specific attachments	At around seven or eight months, babies begin to miss key people in their lives and show signs of distress when those people are absent, e.g. crying when they leave the room. Most babies also seem to have developed one particularly strong attachment – often to the mother. Babies also show a wariness of strangers even when in the presence of their 'key people'. This wariness may quickly develop into fear if the stranger makes some form of direct contact with the baby, e.g. by touching them.
From 8 months onwards	Multiple attachments	After making specific attachments, babies then go on to form multiple attachments. This is an important part of their socialisation process. They remain, however, anxious in the company of strangers and will increasingly become distressed when left alone with a stranger.

Separation anxiety

The term 'separation anxiety' is used to describe how babies and young children react when they are not able to be with their parents or other adult attachment. Separation anxiety can cause long-term emotional damage to young children. This is why it is good practice for children to have settling-in periods so that they can form an attachment with a key person before they start at a setting.

Stages of separation anxiety

Stage	Features
Protest	Children may cry, struggle to escape, kick and show anger.
Despair	Children show calmer behaviour, almost as though they have accepted the separation. They may be withdrawn and sad. Comfort behaviour such as thumb sucking or rocking may be shown.
Detachment	When children are not reunited for a long period of time, e.g. absent parent due to family breakdown, detachment occurs. Children may appear to be 'over' the separation. The child is actually coping by trying to 'forget' the relationship – hence the title 'detachment'. The effects of detachment may be long lasting. To protect themselves from being hurt, children may choose not to get close to others or trust them in case they too abandon them.

Case study

Aziz is two years old. He lives with his mother. While he has played with other children and been in the company of other adults, he has never been looked after by anyone other than his mother. His mother has tried a few times to leave him at a crèche, but each time he has screamed continually until she has returned. Aziz's mother feels that Aziz would benefit from going to a preschool. She is very worried about how he will cope.

Aziz's mother is right to be concerned. He has already experienced separation anxiety and so is likely to do again unless a new attachment is formed with a key person. This will take some time as, apart from his mother, it would appear that he has not formed many close attachments. If settling is taken slowly and the key person creates a bond with Aziz, he should be able to make the transition. A good tip will be for Aziz's mother to gradually withdraw so that, little by little, Aziz becomes used to being alone with his key person.

IN PRACTICE

There are many facets to attachment theory which will affect our work with children:

- **Supporting parents**

Wherever we can, it is important to support parents. Happy, confident parents are more likely to provide the positive care that babies and young children need. This might mean signposting parents to self-help groups, parenting courses or encouraging them to gain professional support.

- **Providing a strong key person and settling-in system**

The effects of separation anxiety can be long lasting. It is important, therefore, to provide children with a strong attachment or key person. This attachment needs to be in place before parents leave their children.

- **Warm, consistent and sensitive responses**

All adults, but especially children's key persons, need to show warm, consistent and sensitive responses towards the child.

- **Time to build and maintain key person relationships**

It is important that children have sufficient time with their key person both in the early days, but also later on. Some settings use group times for this, but actually many children need and benefit from time alone with their key person.

Self-identity and self-esteem

Hand in hand with attachment and also with links to operant conditioning, children's emerging self-identity can also play a part in their behaviour. From very early on in life, children are given messages about what they are like. These messages come from a variety of sources including parents, family members and other key adults in children's lives. They can be very subtle, e.g. disappointment, anger or pleasure in an adult's facial expression. Children can also pick up on the tone of voice or later what is either said directly to them or about them. These messages are all important in forming children's self-identity. It takes years before self-identity and later self-esteem is fully formed, but early messages gained from those around them start to influence children's responses. A child who regularly hears that they are 'good' may increasingly try to please adults. In the same way, a child who develops a reputation of being difficult will develop behaviours accordingly. This is one of the reasons why it is good practice to avoid making global statements about children but instead only comment on their actions. 'Stop it. You are a pain!' is very different from 'Stop it. You are making a mess.'

Self-identity and adults' expectations

As self-identity is developed by watching others and learning from experience what others think of you, children's identity is therefore linked to adults' expectations. If adults have expectations that children cannot meet, there is a danger that children may learn from the adults' reaction that they have failed in some way. If this occurs on a regular basis, children may start to internalise that they are in some way failing. This can cause a child to have lower levels of confidence. On the other hand, if adults' expectations are fair and when children meet them, there is a positive response, children may grow in confidence. Sometimes, adults can have low expectations of children. They may not see their children as capable and so they may not allow them to become independent and autonomous. This can lead children to feeling less competent and more dependent on adults.

Case study

Ali's father has high hopes for him. He regularly tells his son that he must be the best. Although Ali is only three years old, his father wants him to say and write the letters of the alphabet. Ali tries his hardest, but often makes mistakes. His father grumbles and is cross with him. His father rarely says 'well done'. At the childminder, Ali often looks anxious. He often asks if he has been good or whether he has done well.

Ali's father wants him to do well and his intentions are well-meaning. The danger is that Ali may not gain confidence in his own abilities if he regularly feels that he has not measured up to his father's expectations. The childminder can help by providing information for Ali's father about typical stages in development and the link between confidence and achievement. When Ali is in the setting, he may benefit from doing some activities that are easy for him to achieve so that he can feel more successful.

Gender

A major part of self-identity comes from gender. Or, in reality, what other people expect of your gender. There is plenty of research to suggest that adults change how they speak and also how they respond to children according to the gender of the child. In general terms, girls are expected to be more placid and amenable and boys are meant to be active and harder to manage. Some clothes actually display messages that reinforce these gender expectations: 'Here comes trouble' on a boy's t-shirt as opposed to 'Pretty as a peach' for girls. There are many ways in which children will start to pick up on the messages associated with gender.

Why has this girl chosen to wear this outfit?

TOYS AND PLAY OPPORTUNITIES

Toys and play opportunities often build on these adult expectations of gender. Toys and play opportunities for boys often encourage exploration and invention, but some also condone aggression. Monsters, dinosaurs with sharp teeth and superheroes that fight are examples of the way in which boys are subtly given the message that aggression may be tied to masculinity.

Few toys for girls encourage the same level of exploration and invention. While toys marketed for boys may include construction which is open ended, for girls the equivalent is often craft kits. The kits usually do not allow for exploration, but instead encourage instruction-following. Toys designed for girls also promote nurturing language but often require them to be physically more still. Expectations that boys can sit, listen and enjoy activities such as sharing books or doing craft kits are often lower than for girls. In the same way, in some settings there is also an acceptance that girls do not 'do' construction or science-based activities.

In addition, at home, there may be some parental pressure for children, especially boys, not to play with certain toys. Some research shows that some fathers are often very concerned about their son's masculinity. They may tell a boy to stop nursing a doll and instead offer another toy. Dressing up in particular clothes, especially ones that appear feminine, may also be frowned upon.

How this might influence children's self-identity and development

Playing with gendered toys for long periods is likely to shape not only children's development but also their self-identity. Firstly, each type of play will support a range of different skills. Where children spend more time on one type of play, the brain will set up stronger connections and so children will increasingly become competent in that play. Where children start to close down the range of toys and play opportunities that they experience, they are likely to miss out on some key skills. In general terms, it is thought that girls miss out on spatial awareness and exploration while boys miss out on language and some aspects of fine motor development. Over time, if children are weak in certain areas as a result of lack of exposure to the skill, they are likely to come to the conclusion that they are 'no good' at kicking a football or drawing and painting. They may also ascribe their lack of skill in the play opportunity or activity to their gender: 'this is something that girls can't do'. Interestingly, children's lack of interest in certain activities can then reinforce adults' beliefs about what boys and girls want to play with.

GENDER AND ADULTS' RESPONSES

When it comes to how adults respond to children's behaviour, there are also clear differences. Many adults believe that they treat all the children the same, but any boisterous behaviour from girls is curbed sooner than the equivalent for boys. Girls are often expected to wait patiently and show less demanding behaviour. In some settings, there is also a feeling that boys' behaviour is inevitable as 'after all, boys will be boys'. Lower expectations of boys' behaviour can impact on the development of some boys' self-regulation. They may learn to show aggression when frustrated or expect immediate gratification.

Adults are also likely to have unequal expectations of children's development. This is worrying as while individual children may show different patterns of development, there are not separate measures for boys and girls. One important myth worth busting is that boys are likely to be delayed with their language. As language plays an important role in self-regulation as well as other social skills, the expectation that boys will be slower to pick up language is problematic. Provided that boys and girls have the same opportunities to interact, unless a child has a language disorder or learning difficulty, there should be no differences in their language acquisition. Unfortunately, it would appear that some boys are not getting the same opportunities to develop their language as girls – hence why there are discrepancies between boys' and girls' language scores.

Case study

Max's parents say that he is a 'proper boy'. Max is four years old. At home his time is divided between playing with his tablet and being outdoors playing football or using his trike. He is quite a fussy eater and his mum finds it easier to give him food when he is watching television. In the nursery, Max always chooses to be outdoors and he loves pretending to be a superhero with his friends. He is rarely seen in the book corner. Recently, the nursery carried out a language audit. They were shocked to find out just how little time some children actually spent engaged in sustained talking and listening. They also measured children's vocabulary. Max's vocabulary was weaker than expected. As a result, the nursery has changed some of its practices. Key persons are encouraged to spend longer with targeted children and there has been a focus on one-to-one story sharing. As a result, Max has started to be more interested in books. Max's parents are starting to borrow books from the nursery. They were surprised that he was so interested as they thought that he would not enjoy them.

It is great that the nursery has taken the time to audit language levels and the amount of sustained interaction in their setting. The steps they have taken may change some boys' perceptions about reading and books. Sharing books is a key way in which children's vocabulary can be built and also allows for sustained talk. Reading books is sometimes seen as being a 'girl' activity by some parents and so it is not surprising that, up until now, it was not an activity that Max's parents offered. It would be useful for the nursery to share some strategies with his parents about Max's fussy eating with the view that mealtimes at home become more sociable. This is because mealtimes appear to be very helpful at supporting the family unit as well as having beneficial effects on language.

CHECKPOINTS

There is plenty to unpick about gender in relation to children's development and behaviour. This is a hot topic, but worthy of significant discussion.

* How often have you heard terms such as 'proper boy' or 'real boy'? What does this mean for the type of activities that children might choose?
* How many of your play opportunities and toys reinforce gender messages?
* Are there toys, books or images in your setting that subtly promote aggression?
* Do boys gain more attention than girls in your setting?
* Do you have the same expectations of boys' and girls' behaviour?
* Do you challenge adults', including parents', comments relating to gender expectations?
* Are boys given equal opportunities for high-quality and sustained interaction?

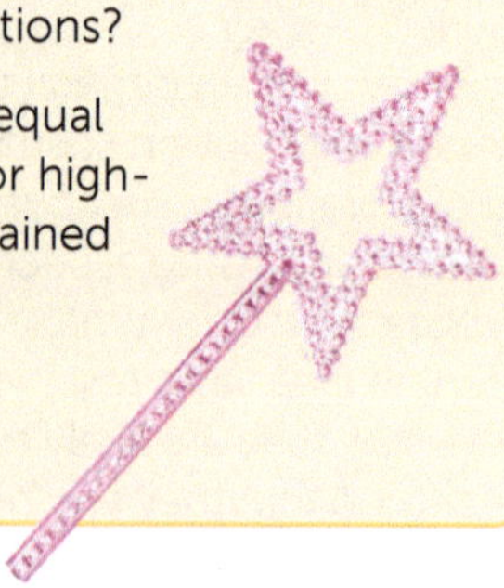

Temperament

We know that children's behaviour is closely tied to their direct experiences, adults' expectations, attachment and also their age and stage of development. However, it is worth recognising that temperamental traits can also play a part in how children respond to different situations. Parents, in particular, will often have recognised some elements of their children's temperament such as how their child reacts to new situations and people.

Research on children's temperament is ongoing, but there is some evidence to suggest that temperamental traits can be recognisable in early childhood. It is important to tread carefully as children do develop over time according to their experiences and interactions with adults and others. Several temperamental traits have been explored by a range of researchers, and it can be worth thinking about these when trying to understand individual children's reactions. By considering children's temperamental traits, adults can then adapt the environment and support children in order that any negative aspects of temperamental traits can be moderated.

Activity level

Some babies and young children seem to be very physically active whilst others are more passive.

Approach/positive emotionality

This trait is about how positively babies and children react to new situations, events and people. Some babies, for example, may immediately enjoy seeing a puppet for the first time.

Inhibition and anxiety

This is the level at which children respond to new situations and people with fear. Babies and children showing high levels of this trait may appear fearful or shy.

Negative emotionality/irritability/anger

This is a trait that looks at how children cope with frustration and how easily they become irritated and show anger.

Effortful control/task persistence

Very early on, some babies and children show high levels of attention and persistence. This trait can be helpful in developing self-regulation.

IN PRACTICE

Children's temperaments may well affect their responses in a setting. It can be worth looking at the different traits and considering individual children in the light of them. A child who finds sitting still difficult and who is constantly being told off for climbing may be a child who has a tendency to be active. In the same way, a child who is always reluctant to try out a sensory activity may be a child who is particularly anxious and so finds some sensations quickly overwhelming.

Children's temperaments may also mean that some children may not be very extrovert and friendly. They may frown rather than smile and this may impact on how easily they make friends. It may also affect adults' responses towards them.

CHECKPOINTS

* Do you talk to parents about their child's temperament and how it affects their day-to-day responses at home?
* Can you identify children who are not as positive and friendly as other children? How do you ensure that these children feel valued and are included by others?
* Are staff aware that they may need to adapt routines, activities and approaches to meet the individual characteristics of children?

Case study

Ava is four years old. The childminder is concerned about how anxious she becomes when there are any changes to the routine. She is reluctant to try out new activities and actively dislikes anything that is loud or sensory. The childminder has noted that once Ava has adjusted to whatever is new, she is usually fine. She is otherwise a smiley and popular child. Ava's parents say that since Ava was little, this has always been the case. They explain that weaning in particular was difficult because Ava would spit out any foods that were unfamiliar. Over time, they have learnt to adapt their approach. They tend to allow Ava more time to adjust to new things.

It is likely that Ava's reluctance to try out new things may be temperamental given that her parents noted this in her when she was a baby. Their approach of taking things slowly and being ready to adapt is an effective one. Rushing or becoming irritated is only likely to exacerbate Ava's tendency to be anxious. Over time and with support, Ava is likely to find it easier to cope with new situations or events. Adults will be able to remind her of how she has been successful in the past and this strategy can build self-confidence.

Chapter 3

Factors affecting children's behaviour and responses

In this section, we look at some of the factors that might affect some of children's day-to-day behaviour as well as reasons why children may not show age-related expectations.

I have divided the factors into four categories:

- Basic needs
- Stress
- Stimulation
- Developmental or medical factors.

Basic needs

There are a few basic needs which, if not met, are likely to influence children's behaviour. Sometimes, making sure that these needs are addressed can make a significant difference to children's ability to be with others.

Tiredness

As we have seen, self-regulation is one of the skills that children need to acquire in order to be with others. When children are tired, their already limited ability to self-regulate is seriously impaired. This can result in 'explosive' outbursts, tantrums and aggression towards others. In addition, being tired can also affect children's ability to stay focused on any activity, even something that they usually enjoy. This means that it is not uncommon for children to show signs of hyperactivity, e.g. running around and tipping things out.

BEING WITH OTHERS IS TIRING

It is always worth remembering that children in groups will become more tired than if they were at home. This is because interactions and play with others is stimulating, providing the brain with constant information to process. By the end of a session or a day, most children will be very tired, especially if they are in a noisy, lively environment.

RECOGNISING TIREDNESS

It is important to monitor individual children's levels of tiredness. If tiredness is picked up quickly, we can re-adjust the environment and also the expectations of the child. A tired child might need to play in a quiet area or be supported to tidy up.

It is always a good idea to start appraising a child when they first come into the setting. Are they alert? What do parents say about their day so far? In addition, individual children show that they are becoming tired through physical signs. Some children become pale, others start twiddling their hair or rocking.

HOW MUCH SLEEP?

It is helpful to produce a guide for parents as to how much sleep children typically need. While there are likely to be individual differences, it is important to pick up on those children who are significantly under-sleeping and so are finding it hard to cope with the demands of being with others.

THE ROLE OF NAPS

When parents are finding it hard to get their children to bed, it is not illogical for them to assume that naps are the cause of the problem. While long naps taken late into the afternoon may cause a problem, overall, naps can actually be the solution. This is because children who become overtired can find it hard to relax and settle down to sleep at night. Naps can also help children cope as the day wears on and they become tired as a result of additional stimulation.

Physical activity and being outdoors

Many adults underestimate children's need for physical activity and its link to children's behaviour. Children's bodies and also their brains need to be stimulated and making physical movements is essential. Being physically active helps children's concentration, enables them to gain a sense of self-efficacy and supports their overall wellbeing. The guideline for children (0–5 years), once they are walking, is that they should spend three hours during the day being active. This includes light physical activity such as walking or standing as well as more energetic activity such as running, jumping or climbing.

As well as focusing on physical activity, it is also worth thinking about how much time children spend outdoors. This is because children respond very differently when outdoors. This may be because play opportunities tend to be more open ended, but also because children are able to move faster and further than indoors.

Q

We have a three-year-old who comes at 7.30 am and leaves at 6 pm. Her parents are insistent that she should not have a nap. By three o'clock in the afternoon, her behaviour starts to deteriorate. She has tantrums or snatches from other children.

It is clear that this is a child who needs a nap, but whose parents may also be struggling with sleep at home. See if you can talk to parents about the importance of sleep (and naps) in preventing children from becoming overtired. It may be that you will need to signpost parents to sources of information and help as they may be struggling at home with a bedtime routine. You may also need to remind them that you have a duty of care towards their child and that if she becomes very tired, it will be in her best interests to let her have a nap. To avoid conflict around naps, consider developing a 'sleep policy' so that parents know your position on naps before they join your setting.

A

Q

We have a group of mainly girls who say that they don't want to go outside. Should we be forcing them?

An interesting change has taken place in children's lives in recent times. Traditionally, children spent a lot of time outdoors playing, but now most children spend more time indoors. For some children, it no longer feels natural to be outdoors. Start off by thinking about what there is to do for these children. It may be that the toys and resources do not appeal to them or that they are not sure how to use them. You could also think about a small activity that is adult led that the children might find interesting, e.g. hiding a teddy outdoors and seeing if they can find it. It is also important to think about adult attitudes towards going outdoors. If adults are positive and enthusiastic, children usually pick up on this. There are so many things that children can do and enjoy including gardening and bug spotting as well as using resources such as balls and parachutes.

A

CHECKPOINTS

* Have you noticed that on days when the weather is bad and children are not so physically active, their behaviour changes?
* Where do most of the incidents that require adults to intervene take place – indoors or outdoors?
* Consider identifying children who have arrived by car or pushchair and encourage early physical activity on arrival.
* How do you monitor children's level of physical activity during the session?
* What information do you provide for parents about the importance of physical activity?
* Is there are a varied selection of resources, toys and activities for children to try out?
* How enthusiastic are adults about being outdoors?

Children need three hours of physical activity a day

Hunger and food

Another basic need which can affect children's behaviour is hunger. Children who are hungry may become more emotional or impulsive. Toddlers in particular are more likely to have tantrums if they are hungry. There has also been some research to demonstrate the links between concentration and food. Regular mealtimes seem to aid concentration and also help children's learning.

In addition to making sure that children do not become over-hungry, it is also important to consider the link between nutrition and food. While there is controversy about whether additives can change children's behaviour, it is clear that good nutrition plays a role in children's healthy development.

CHECKPOINTS

* Have you tracked whether more incidents take place before mealtimes?
* Are there any individual children who seem to be affected adversely by hunger?
* Are you knowledgeable about the latest guidelines for food and nutrition for young children?

Stress

As with adults, children can react badly to stress. This is then reflected in their responses. In the same way that some adults can feel stress more acutely than other adults, the same is true with children. There are many reasons why stress may occur. In this part, we will look at:

- **Settling in and attachment**
- **Stress in the environment**
- **Changes in children's lives**
- **Safeguarding.**

Settling in and attachment

We saw in the previous section that attachment can play a significant part in children's emotional and social development. Moving from home to the early years setting is stressful for children unless they are completely secure. Attention-seeking behaviours and behaviours borne from

frustration and anger may occur if children are stressed in addition to the classic signs of separation anxiety (see page 29). Young children need a strong attachment to at least one adult in the setting in order for them to cope. A strong attachment is important in helping to reduce children's stress levels. This is partly because when children have a strong attachment, they are more likely to seek physical comfort such as holding hands or requesting a hug. This physical contact is a powerful way of reducing stress levels.

The importance of attachment on children's emotional and social development means that in England, for example, it is a legal requirement for settings to provide each child with a key person. Attachments between key person and child take time to develop and should be in place before a child starts at a setting. It is also important to think about how much time children spend with their key person. In general terms, children who are under three, new to a setting or do not have much language will need more time with their key person. When this is not available, children are more likely to show challenging behaviours.

CHECKPOINTS

* Are your settling-in processes allowing children to develop a sufficiently strong relationship with their key person?
* How do you assess the quality of the key person–child relationship?
* Are there any children who have not developed a strong relationship with their key person?
* How much time do children routinely spend with their key person?
* Is the adult–child ratio in your setting sufficient to meet the attachment needs of children?

Stress in the environment

It is easy to forget that for some children, a large, busy and noisy environment will actually be stressful for them. It is one reason why some children will prefer to go into small spaces such as the home corner. It is also why children will seek out their key persons or, as they develop further, their friends. As adults, we may not always appreciate how much noise, movement and distraction is occurring within our setting unless we actively reflect upon it.

CHECKPOINTS

* Have you ever recorded the noise level in your setting?
* Do you have resources that will deaden sound, e.g. carpets, soft furnishings?
* Can you identify individual children who prefer calmer activities and environments?

CONSISTENT ADULTS

Children can find it very stressful if adults' responses are very unpredictable, e.g. sunny and relaxed one day but irritable another. While most adults working with children will have their good days and their more challenging days, it is essential that the impact on children is minimal. This is requisite when working professionally with children. For children whose home lives are unpredictable, it is particularly important that they are with consistent adults.

It is also important how adults deal with incidents and challenges. The term 'spill-over effect' is used in this context. The idea behind the 'spill-over effect' is that the way that adults talk to other children or react to incidents can affect other children who are nearby but not involved. A good example of this would be an adult who is irritated because a trike will not fit into the shed. The adult kicks the trike in frustration. If this small act is noticed by the children, it is likely to increase their stress levels. In the same way, children can feel very uncomfortable when they can hear or see an adult becoming cross with another child. It is also worth noting that adults who are very loud and boisterous in their style may in some cases be overwhelming for children who are particularly prone to stress.

CHECKPOINTS

* Are all adults aware that they need to be calm in their manner at all times?
* How do adults support each other to create a positive work environment?

ADULT–CHILD RATIOS

In some settings, the cause of some unwanted behaviour is linked to insufficient adults being available for children. We have seen already that young children do need plenty of attention and also are likely to need the reassuring presence of a key person. When there are not enough adults on the ground, attention can be in short supply and so children react to this. In addition, adults themselves can become stressed which can affect the consistency of their responses. It is worth noting here that the legal adult–child ratios are minimum ratios. They are based on all the children showing typical development. Group settings that are very large in terms of physical space and/or have many children who are not showing age-related development are likely to need an increased adult–child ratio. In some cases, a lack of adult availability may be seen just at certain times of the day or session, e.g. mealtimes, start of the day or end of the session.

Q

I work in a school nursery. We have a working ratio of 1:13 for our three-year-olds and 1:4 for our two-year-olds. We have both age groups together in a very large classroom and a huge outdoor area. At times, I feel that we are very stretched especially when a child's nappy needs changing and an adult is out of the room. Many of the children come in with low levels of development. On some days, I know that I have not spoken to all of my key children. We have asked the headteacher for more staff, but we have been told that we are in ratio. What else can we do?

This is not an unusual problem. Some headteachers and managers do not always realise that the legal ratios are minimum ones. It is worth presenting a case on paper as to why the current ratios are not sufficient in terms of ensuring children's health and safety, but also supporting their development. A three-part format can be useful: begin by outlining the current concerns that you have, e.g. that an accident may occur because there are insufficient staff or that children's progress is being compromised because they are not having sufficient interaction. Then, explain in detail what is needed to remedy the situation. Finally, outline the likely consequences of inaction, e.g. a poor inspection report or a serious accident.

A

CHECKPOINTS

- How stretched are adults at certain times of the day?
- Is some children's behaviour linked to the routine of the setting?
- Is the adult–child ratio sufficient to meet the developmental needs of the children?
- Have you looked at how adults are used to ensure the maximum amount of time is spent with individual or very small groups of children?

ROUTINES

Routines can help children feel safe and secure and so they are important in reducing stress in children. Having said that, if routines are not developmentally appropriate, they can actually backfire and become a repeated source of stress. It is worth thinking about whether any of the routines in your setting are repeatedly sources of conflict or unwanted behaviour. If so, it may be that the routines are not working for either individual children or groups of children. Some routines that were developed in very established settings may have been fine at the time, but longer session lengths or the addition of younger children can mean that they may no longer work. Examples of routines that commonly become sources of stress in group settings include circle time, registration and story time. This is likely to be because they require children to sit and be fairly inactive. Developmentally, this is often problematic for children under four. In addition, some routines can restrict the amount of time children spend outdoors. It is worth noting that time outdoors can be hugely beneficial for children and is usually associated with children feeling more relaxed.

These children know what to expect next

Q

We are a preschool and have been doing circle time for a number of years. It is part of our routine. We normally do circle time just after snack. One adult leads it and the others support the children. In our last inspection, it was noted that not all the children were engaged and that some were bored. What can we do to improve our circle time?

From time to time, all routines need to be taken off the shelves and dusted down. What was working before may no longer be so relevant. There are three factors that affect children's ability to enjoy and engage in circle time. The first is children's age, the second is the level of children's language and the third is group size. The chances are that you are now taking younger children and also have more children that have lower levels of speech and language. From what you describe, your group size is also likely to be too large. There is no obligation to do circle time. Instead, consider splitting the children into smaller groups to do different things with an adult. One group could have a story, another might sing rhymes or a song and a final group could do a nature walk outdoors, for example. This way you would still have a routine, but one that works better for the children.

A

CHECKPOINTS

* When did you last reflect upon the effectiveness of your routine?
* Consider going through each part of your routine and thinking about why you do it and whether or not it works for all of the children.

Changes in children's lives

It is said that children are very adaptable. Unfortunately, this is not quite true. Young children find change very difficult even if it is only a case of someone else picking them up. Anger, attention-seeking behaviour and clinginess are common in children who are coping with changes. Interestingly, children often do not know that how they are feeling or acting is linked to the changes in their lives. Some changes are temporary in nature and children will settle down fairly quickly, provided that adults are sensitive and provide some level of continuity. The list shows common examples of temporary changes:

- **A different person dropping off or collecting the child.**
- **Family member or friend visiting at home.**
- **Key person is away on holiday or on a training course.**
- **Child has been ill.**
- **Short-term arguments or tension at home.**
- **Changes in the setting, e.g. going on an outing.**
- **Absence of a close friend from the setting.**
- **Changes to the days for sessions.**

SIGNIFICANT CHANGES

Significant changes are those which will change elements of the child's life in some way. This includes moving home or setting as well as changes to family relationships. In particular, children find it hard to cope when people that they feel strongly towards are no longer available for them. This may occur because of a bereavement or family breakdown. They can also find the introduction of a new adult or other children difficult which may occur when a new partner comes in to a parent's life.

DELAYED REACTIONS

Some children appear at the time to cope well with change but later on start to show adverse reactions intermittently. This is often the case, for example, with the arrival of a sibling or after a bereavement. In some cases, children show reactions. They may appear to be fine on some days or weeks but at other times show behaviours such as aggression or tearfulness.

Painting can be one way in which children can express their emotions

SUPPORTING CHILDREN WITH CHANGES

Ensuring there are supportive adults around children during times of change can make a significant difference to the outcome. There are several ways in which we can help children:

Preparation – Wherever possible, it is important for children to be prepared for the changes that are due to occur. This might include explaining what is going to happen, telling a story or using role play.

Continuity – Ideally, when children are going through an upheaval, their key person or other strong attachment will need to take on a greater role and thus help them to feel safe. Keeping to some routines can also be helpful so that children can still see that there is a pattern to their lives. It is helpful if the routines around certain times are also maintained, e.g. children lay the table for lunch or music is put on before a nap.

Naming emotions – Children often do not have the language to explain how they are feeling. They may not connect their actions to their emotions. It is helpful if adults label the emotions.

Flexibility – While consistency is important, adults also have to be sensitive and flexible in their approach. Some children may show signs of regression, e.g. want to be dressed or fed. While typically children might be encouraged to be independent, being flexible might mean helping the child and so making them feel nurtured. It may also be important to be flexible in how incidents of behaviour are dealt with although it is important that some boundaries are maintained.

Expression – Having sensory materials available including musical instruments can be helpful as children can find relief in expressing their emotions with these resources. Some children may also use role play as a way of processing what has happened in their lives.

Following children's lead – Where children have had very significant changes to their lives, it is important to follow their lead when it comes to talking about what has happened. It is also normal for children to 'flit' between emotions, e.g. cry violently but then play twenty minutes later.

Signposting and gaining more information – The following websites offer advice on supporting a child through significant change in their lives: **www.winstonswish.org.uk, www.familylives.org.uk** and **www.bbc.co.uk/cbeebies/grownups/helping-your-child-prepare-for-an-operation**.

Q

We have a child in our setting whose mother died of cancer a couple of months ago. The child is four years old. At the time, the child appeared to be coping well, but recently they appear to be very angry and often become aggressive. We are not sure what we should do.

The grieving process is a journey and children will reach different stages at different times. The first stage of grief is often characterised by disbelief. It could be that when the child appeared to be coping, they were in this stage. It is worth talking to family members and seeing how things are going at home. It may be that the child may need some professional support. In any case, it will be useful for you to gain some advice from one of the child bereavement organisations. The child will benefit from some calm and consistent routines as well as opportunities to be with their key person. In terms of dealing with aggressive behaviours, children need to hear that while it is fine for them to feel anger or sadness, it is not acceptable to hit out at others.

A

Practical ways to reduce stress

There are some simple, but effective ways in which we can reduce stress for children.

PHYSICAL CONTACT

Being touched, hugged or cuddled by someone who is emotionally close can be helpful in reducing stress. This means that young children are likely to benefit from holding an adult's hand or having a hug or cuddle. Many young children will instinctively seek out this physical contact, but you may also need to offer it to slightly older children. Whilst physical contact is extremely effective in reducing anxiety, it only works if the child is comfortable with the adult. If this is not the case, physical contact can actually increase anxiety and stress.

MINI-ROUTINES

It is worth creating mini-routines for children who are not coping. The idea of a mini-routine is that it creates additional structures for children within the overall routine of the setting and that is guided by an adult that the child trusts and likes. A mini-routine might include greeting the child at the start of the session and then doing a simple activity with the adult until the child is looking more relaxed.

CALMING ENVIRONMENTS

For children who find being in a group setting stressful, it is worth looking for ways of creating a calmer and quieter environment. This might mean adults talking more quietly, looking for ways to cut down background noise and reviewing the environment to create areas where there is less movement and activity. It can also be worth choosing calm colours such as grey, pale blue or beige for walls and ensuring that displays are minimal and colour coordinated.

Safeguarding issues

One of the unfortunate factors that impact on children's behaviour is abuse. Children who are subject to neglect or any other type of abuse may often signal this through their behaviour. The job of all professionals is to consider carefully whether abuse could be the underlying reason why children are showing atypical age or stage behaviour. Many serious case reviews that are held after a child has died or been seriously injured show that opportunities to identify and potentially stop the abuse were missed. This happens for a variety of reasons, but one of them is often the failure of professionals to consider whether there is a link and also to question carefully parents' or carers' explanations. Most people working in early years are wonderful, kind and could not countenance hurting a child. This, in some ways, makes it hard for them to believe that a parent, another staff member or even an older child could be abusing a child that they work with.

RECOGNISING FAMILIES AT RISK

In some cases, we may recognise that a parent is struggling with their child's behaviour. Signs such as rough handling, shouting or threatening should not be ignored however uncomfortable it makes us feel. When public standards of parenting are low, one has to wonder what will happen behind closed doors. It is important, therefore, to step in and see if you can support the parent in some way or signpost help. If you are concerned for the welfare of the child, you should always raise these concerns.

CHECKPOINTS

- Do you work with or have contact numbers for services that can support parents?
- Are you confident that you could step in to help a parent that is not coping?
- Do you know who to contact if you had concerns about a child's welfare?

Stimulation

The layout of an environment and also what there is for children to do within it can significantly affect the responses of children. Children are hungry learners and explorers and need stimulation. While most practitioners recognise that children need stimulation, quite often they underestimate what this might look like in practice. This is because it is easy to forget that many children today spend quite long periods of time within a single setting. A child in a day care setting will on average have spent at least 8,000 hours there, while sessional children can easily clock up 2,000 hours. This means that the sand tray or the toy cars that once fascinated a two-year-old may no longer be as exciting after a thousand hours of looking at them. While tweaking these activities can work by, for example, colouring the water, or putting tubes out for the cars, for some children this is simply not enough. The term 'continuous provision' is often used in settings, but it is important to reflect on whether for some children who have already 'been there, done it' the term really means 'continuous boredom'. When this happens, children are likely to try to use the materials creatively but in ways that adults did not intend, e.g. climbing up the chute of the slide or chopping off the hair of the dolls. One sign that often indicates that hour by hour, there is not sufficient stimulation on offer is when children become hugely excited by new equipment or by an interesting adult-led activity.

CHECKPOINTS

* How much time do children typically spend in your setting?
* Do you ever think that children have 'outgrown' your setting?
* How do you ensure that there are enough new opportunities for children to explore and learn from?
* Do the types of equipment, resources and activities significantly change from day to day and during the actual session?
* Are adult-led activities planned that will sufficiently challenge children?

Interesting adult-led activities can stimulate children

Risk and thrill

Allied to stimulation is the need for children, as they become older, to explore risk and thrill. Some of the behaviours that are unsafe and have to be stopped are often linked to children wanting to experience a 'thrill'. This might mean walking on a high wall or hitting a tree with a stick. Few settings plan safe activities that will give children the feelings of risk and thrill. This results in children manufacturing them. It is therefore worth thinking about safe activities that will help children explore this. This might include games such as 'dodge ball' or games that involve chasing or hiding. Interestingly, some early years settings have adopted forest school activities. They often report how activities such as helping to build a fire or even whittling wood can help older children in particular.

CHECKPOINTS

- Do you plan activities to give older children opportunities to safely explore risk and thrill?
- Could you consider making a list of quick games that could be offered as alternatives when children are playing in ways that are not safe?
- Is your outdoor area sufficiently challenging?

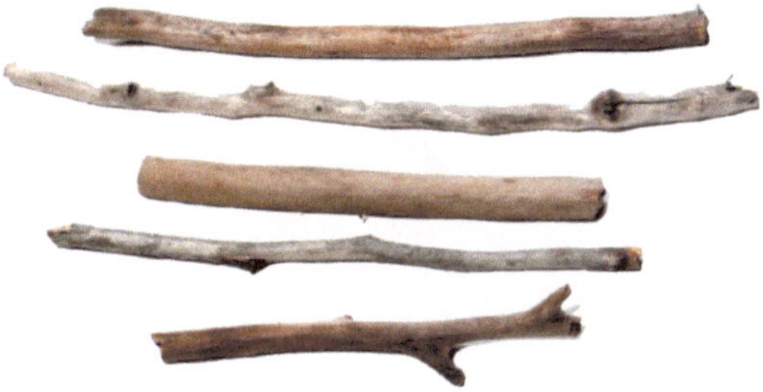

Developmental or medical factors

Children's behaviour can be linked sometimes to developmental factors.

Recognising atypical patterns of development

For some children, their behaviour is linked to an atypical pattern of development. It may be that a child has a social and communication difficulty or a learning difficulty. While it is not the role of the early years practitioner to diagnose, it is important that any atypical development is recognised. Prompt referrals can have a significant impact on the quality of children's and their families' lives. This is because once a child's needs are known, it becomes easier to understand how best to work with them. In many cases, we will need to make adjustments to our provision and ways of working.

CHECKPOINTS

- How often is children's development monitored?
- What resources and support do you have in place to recognise atypical patterns of development?
- How do you help parents to recognise that a referral may be needed?

Speech and language development

One of the most significant developmental factors affecting children's ability to self-regulate is their language development. Interestingly, it is one reason why most three-year-olds respond so differently to the same situation than they did when they were two years old. There are several reasons why language is important:

EXPRESSION

The ability to express yourself and for others to understand your meaning makes a significant difference to children's levels of frustration and sense of self-efficacy. Self-efficacy is about feeling a sense of competence.

UNDERSTANDING WHAT IS HAPPENING AND WHY

Once children have strong levels of language, they can start to understand what is happening and the reasons for it, e.g. 'You need to get your coat on as it's raining outdoors.' They can also use their language to connect different experiences, e.g. 'Walk, don't run. Do you remember how Samuel fell the other day and hurt himself?'

LANGUAGE FOR SELF-CONTROL

One of the ways that we control ourselves is through conscious thought. You may 'tell yourself' not to be provoked by the actions of another or that another person is forgetful because they are not feeling well. This level of language use is sometimes known as 'inner speech'. In children, this develops alongside 'external speech'.

Monitoring language levels

It is important to monitor children's language levels and to consider whether difficulties with speech and language are the cause of children's frustration. Typically, children who have lower levels of language or are hard to understand will be more impulsive.

Language development plays an important role in children's development

While responding to their behaviour at the time will be necessary, unless they can be helped to communicate, they will still continue to find it hard to cope. It is worth not only increasing the amount of interaction children are getting but referring children for an assessment. It can also be worth using more visual ways of helping children to communicate, e.g. signs, photos.

EAL children

While children who are new to English do not have a language delay or difficulty, they may become frustrated because they can no longer use verbal means to communicate. This can lead to children becoming isolated and frustrated which in turn can impact on their behaviour. It is important that children have sufficient time with their key person to build their language but also that visual methods of communication are encouraged.

CHECKPOINTS

- Can you see a link between children who have low levels of language or difficulties with their speech and their ability to self-regulate?
- How do you encourage parents to recognise the link between emotional and social development and language?
- Are you and other adults in the setting aware of typical milestones for speech and language?
- How do you ensure that children with the greatest language need are given the most adult interaction?
- What visual methods do you use to facilitate communication, e.g. body language, signs and photos?

Hearing and vision

It is always worth considering whether children are seeing and hearing well. Left undetected, children can become isolated and also start to show signs of frustration.

GLUE EAR

Glue ear is a form of conductive hearing loss. It is a temporary hearing loss but can significantly reduce children's ability to listen. It is extremely common in young children and can affect how they behave. Glue ear can be difficult to detect as the hearing loss can fluctuate meaning that on some days, a child will hear well, but at other times may have very little hearing. Parents and adults working with children often reach the conclusion that the child is just 'in their own world' or has 'selective hearing'. Glue ear is more common in autumn and winter when children are more prone to colds. It is thought that nearly a quarter of children are affected by it at any one time.

It is important that everyone keeps an eye out for children who may not be fully hearing. If glue ear is suspected, a hearing test will be needed. Sometimes, more than one hearing test is required as the child might be tested during a good period. The following signs are worth watching out for:

- **Muffled speech** – sounds are unclear making it hard to understand the child.
- **Withdrawn** – the child plays alone.
- **Startled** – the child appears startled as they have not heard you approach.
- **Staring at faces** – the child stares at your lips intently as you speak.
- **Aggression** – the child is aggressive with other children.
- **Loud speech** – the child talks loudly and even when prompted finds it hard to moderate tone or volume.
- **Copies others** – the child often seems to copy others after instructions have been given.
- **Varying responses** – sometimes the child appears to respond immediately, but at other times ignores an adult.

Q

Cara is nearly four years old. She has just started at the preschool. She has had several bouts of glue ear that have affected her speech. She talks well, but other children and staff find her hard to understand. At times, she becomes very frustrated when other children do not seem to listen to her. Today, she pushed another child down after a squabble about some dressing up clothes. How should we respond sensitively to this problem?

Glue ear is a condition that affects many children. It is important that the nursery checks whether she is hearing as it may be that she is having another bout of glue ear. Cara may need a referral for an assessment from the speech and language team. To help her speech, it is important that the noise levels in the nursery are low as this will help her hear the sounds and patterns in words. Staff should gain her attention before talking to her and also make eye contact. They can encourage other children to do this. Staff should avoid talking more loudly as this is likely to distort the sounds in words. Cara is likely to show frustrated behaviours at times but these can be managed by making sure that she is supported in her play with others.

A

Chapter 4

Top tips to create a positive environment

We have looked at explanations of how children develop behaviours as well as factors that affect children's responses. Once pulled together, these form the basis of my top tips for early years settings. These are practical tips that, if adults employ, can make it easier for children to cope with the demands of being in early years settings. The idea is to take a proactive approach so that children are not put in a position where unwanted behaviours are likely to occur.

1 Fair expectations, consistency and clear messages

Fair, but not low expectations

We have seen that age and stage is linked to how easily children can self-regulate. Make sure that your expectations are developmentally appropriate for each child that you work with. This means recognising that children under three years will struggle to share and take turns unless helped by an adult. It also means that children under four years will find it hard to wait for long periods and stay still without a distraction. As well as being fair, it is also important not to have low expectations of children and to have some goals for behaviour. Children can often start on the journey of acquiring some skills if supported by adults. For example, a two-year-old may struggle to wait to be served, but may be able to do so if encouraged by an adult and it becomes part of the routine. In addition to having fair and age-related expectations, you should make sure that your expectations are not related to gender, e.g. 'well, he is a boy so what can you expect?' It can also be useful to share age and stage milestones with parents so that they can also understand what might be a fair expectation and also what their role might be in helping their child towards future social skills.

The chart on page 54 show typical stages of development for different age groups as well goals that adults may help children progress towards.

The stage of development and goals for behaviour at different ages

Age	Stage of development	Goals for behaviour
1–2 years	• Actively exploring objects within the environment • No awareness of danger • Copies adults' simple actions • Repeats actions that gain attention from adults • May protest if unable to have what they can see • Has no understanding of ownership	• To play alongside other children for short periods although may try to take others' toys or possessions • To occasionally follow a simple instruction with adult help • To tidy one or two items away as part of a game with an adult, e.g. toys in a bag
2–3 years	• Easily frustrated and may have tantrums if thwarted • May be persistent in wanting objects and harder to distract • Copies actions of others • May insist on immediate attention and be jealous of adult showing attention to others • Will find it hard to wait for things • Active and restless • Little understanding of sharing or taking turns	• To wait for short periods, e.g. at meal times • To take turns when an adult is present and supporting them • To share toys or food with one other with adult help • To play alongside other children and occasionally be co-operative • To sit and share a story with one or two other children for five minutes • To follow simple instructions such as 'Get your coat, please'
3–4 years	• Follows simple routines, e.g. putting on a coat before going outdoors • Able to wait for a short while unless tired • Enjoys being with other children • Can play co-operatively some of the time if not tired • Enjoys helping adults • Occasional tantrums when tired and frustrated • Able to take turns and share some of the time without adult help	• To wait including not interrupting others • To play games with some rules with adult help, e.g. picture lotto • To help to tidy up after they have finished playing with adult sometimes reminding • To share and take turns with resources and toys consistently • To follow instructions of adults most of the time • To show courtesy towards others, e.g. using 'thank you', holding doors open for other when reminded by adults • To talk rather than use actions to express frustration or anger some of the time
4–5 years	• Plays with other children co-operatively and without help from adults • Able to wait for longer periods • Shows understanding for the need to follow rules • Able to take turns and share without adult help unless very tired	• To show thoughtfulness towards others spontaneously • To use words to negotiate, persuade or to express feelings • To tidy up after activities • To show common courtesies towards others without adult reminders which may include greeting others, saying thank you

Make expectations clear

Few young children can second-guess adults' expectations. It is important to help children know what they should be doing by either showing them and/or telling them. Ideally, you should also provide a simple explanation of the reason. Some children will also need you to remind them several times as they may not have the appropriate level of cognitive or language development to retain the information given. Timing can also be important; it is usually better to articulate any expectations at the time and in the situation when it is most relevant to the child.

A proactive and positive approach is essential when working with children

Match face, body language and voice tone

There will be times when adults need to give clear messages to children. This is often to tell them to stop what they are doing, e.g. throwing sand on the floor. As with adults, children pay more attention to body language and facial expression than they do to words. Making sure that your words match up with your body language is therefore essential. If you smile when are you are telling young children to stop an activity, the chances are that they will carry on. This is because the more powerful message is the smile – an encouragement – rather than the words.

Case study

Seren is three years old. She is a happy child, very curious and keen to explore. In a restaurant, despite being given a new toy to look at, Seren has taken her mother's bag and is tipping out all of the things onto the floor. Her mother smiles and gently says, 'Darling, please don't do that. These are mummy's special things.' Seren ignores her mother and carries on. The next day, Seren's mother mentions that Seren is starting to rule the roost at home. She says that the only way that she can 'get through to her' is often by shouting at her.

Seren's stage of development means that she is likely to want to touch and explore things. She is also likely to want plenty of adult attention. In a public place, some parents also feel that they cannot risk a scene and so may give out mixed messages. In this case, it may be that Seren's mother regularly fails to effectively communicate her expectations. Seren is not setting out to deliberately be uncooperative, but her mother's messaging is not sufficiently powerful. This then leads to a situation where the mother becomes frustrated and angry. The nursery could suggest to Seren's mother that she observes how the nursery practitioners use their tone of voice and body language to convey expectations and messages to children.

Consistency matters

Adults need to be consistent with their expectations. Young children find it hard to understand 'exceptions' and so it is not fair for them if one day they are allowed to do something, but not the next. Changes in expectations are particularly difficult for children who are under three years or who have lower levels of language. This is because they may not be able to process the explanation as to why an exception Is happening.

Ideally, there should be consistency in expectations between home and early years setting, but this is often not possible. Having said this, some children seem to be able to move from home to setting and remember the expectations provided that these have been consistent. Within a group setting, the team needs to agree on what really matters and stay consistent.

Q

We have a child whose parent does not believe in discipline. At home, the child seems to be in charge and is never challenged. As a result, this child finds it hard to follow instructions and is often defiant. How can we challenge this behaviour?

While consistency between home and early years setting is the ideal, it often does not happen. The good news is that children can learn to behave differently according to where they are and who they are with. While you could talk to the parent, there is no guarantee that they will change their parenting style although you might like to share with them how consistency of routines and expectations will help their child to develop self-regulation. Instead, focus on creating a warm, positive environment for this child, but with clear, consistent expectations. Remember it will take a while for this child to adapt to being in a group setting, but with time and plenty of positive acknowledgement, the child will start to be more comfortable.

A

Terms and conditions apply

While we want to say 'yes' as many times as possible to children, there will be situations when terms and conditions apply. We may say to children that they can go outside, but they have to put their coat on first. We may be happy for children to play with sand, but terms and conditions apply if sand is thrown at another child. This is sometimes called boundary setting but I quite like the 'terms and conditions apply' phrase. As children become older, it is fair to provide them with an explanation of the terms and conditions and also to let them know what the consequences will be if the terms and conditions are not adhered to. It is important that children learn that if we have said something, we will follow through with it. Having said that, it is key that adults think carefully about the consequences that they are outlining.

Case study

Anna has put out the musical instruments for a group of five children to play with. She has told the children that if they start to argue about the instruments, then they will be put back into the cupboard. After a couple of minutes, there is a little tussle over a drum. Anna tells the children that they must put all the instruments back in the box. She proceeds to put them in the cupboard. Two of the children who were not involved in the squabble, sob and protest that it is not fair.

While it is good that Anna followed through with the consequences, the problem is that she did not think through what was fair for these children. Many children will struggle if they feel that another child has a better resource than them. It would have been better if Anna had allocated instruments to children and then set up a system whereby they swapped. Anna also did not think through the consequences of her terms and conditions. Taking instruments away from children who did not squabble is unjust. The danger is that children are more likely to focus on the unfairness rather than the action of squabbling that led to the instruments being taken away.

2 Accentuate the positive

Creating a positive environment and using positive strategies can make a huge difference to the way children respond.

Notice, praise and acknowledge

Young children need adults to act as guides for them. This means that we need to notice when children are playing well together, waiting for their turn or showing patience with a younger child. Smile and comment so that children learn that this valued behaviour and its effect on others and on themselves can be very significant, e.g. 'Well done for waiting at the door. That means we could keep everyone safe.'

For children who struggle to cope with the demands of being with others, we need to 'catch' their good moments especially if they are starting to develop a negative reputation with other children. As children develop, we might slightly change tack and ask children about how acts of kindness, patience or perseverance make them feel. The aim is that, over time, children learn to praise themselves rather than to look out for external reinforcement.

Keep children enjoyably busy

Children are competent learners. They also have hungry, growing brains. Some incidents of unwanted behaviour take place when children are not engaged in something that is gripping for them. Watch out particularly for situations when children are waiting or do not have anything to do. While some children are quick to entertain themselves, other children may need more direction to get them started. Think carefully about your environment, toys and resources. What is new for children to concentrate on? What will children enjoy doing with an adult during the session?

Be positive

Smiles, plenty of positive attention and jolly reminders can really make a difference to day-to-day behaviour. Where adults are positive in body language and statements, children tend to do well. If something happens, avoid making it personal. Expressions such as 'that was not such a great idea' are better than a personal comment such as 'you are being annoying today'. The latter is not likely to make the child feel confident or valued.

Positive attitudes from adults can help children to show positive behaviours

Fresh starts

When there have been setbacks or difficulties, it is useful to reset the session and the pace, giving a child or children a fresh start. This can be achieved by putting out a new activity, putting on music or physically moving – going outdoors if the incident occurred indoors. When children have had some difficulties, it is also important to help them be successful immediately afterwards. This might mean asking if they would like to help you to lay the table, tidy up or straighten some books. Choose something that will not take much time and that the child is likely to be keen to do. Positively acknowledge the child during the task and make sure that it feels fun.

Step by step

Some children with low levels of self-regulation will need adults to support them and to break down things that are difficult for them into smaller steps. A child who finds it hard to wait their turn will find it hard to wait for six other children to have a turn. Breaking things down into smaller steps will mean that the adult will help the child to wait for just one other child before having their turn. The next time, the child will then wait for two other children before their turn.

3 Be organised!

The organisation and the environment we create around children can really affect their responses. It is important that we are organised and are quick to be proactive and reflective.

Think ahead; put yourself in children's shoes

One way in which you can help children is to put yourself in their shoes when planning the environment and activities. Use your experience of working with individual children and also your knowledge about age and stage to predict their responses. A tablecloth over a table is likely to prompt children to go underneath, while a long sheet of paper on the floor is likely to be walked on by children. By thinking ahead, you can either accommodate children's natural ways of playing or in the case of resources needing to be shared, provide alternative distractions of equal interest. Thinking ahead is particularly important when working with children under three years who will find it harder to regulate their impulses. If they can see something, they will want to have it immediately. If the object or resources is not available for them, they will find it hard to understand this.

Recognise the pinch points

In most settings, there are some key times in the day that I call 'pinch points'. These are the times when adults may feel stretched and where incidents occur. These are often times when there is some routine transition such as going outdoors or home time. Pinch points may also occur when children are becoming tired and their ability to self-regulate is starting to wane. Instead of accepting these as just being difficult, it is worth reflecting on them. A good starting point is to ask yourself whether that bit of the routine is actually necessary. Do all the children need to come and sit down for a register or could it be done differently? If the answer is yes, then consider how it could be done differently to make it either more efficient and/or more enjoyable for children. It may be that children need to get their coats, but could it be done in small groups? Could there be a dressing song?

Remove temptation but provide equivalent distraction

Removing resources or items that are causing an issue can be an important strategy in helping children. There are two situations in which you might decide to do this. Firstly, you may predict that the object or resources will become a source of conflict that will create tension or arguments. Removing these before children notice them will therefore prevent any issues. This is an important strategy to use for children who are low in self-regulation or are just having a bad day! The second situation in which you may remove temptation is when children are doing something or are likely to do something that will be dangerous or cause a conflict. Two children who have found a stick each and are play-fighting may find it hard to stop. Removing the items not as a punishment but as a way of helping children to avoid difficulties is a good strategy. In such situations, it is important to explain why the item is about to be removed and also to provide the children with alternative and equal distraction. This might mean proposing a game such as dodge ball.

Case study

Little Bees nursery has increased the number of children that it is taking. This is creating new challenges for the staff as some of their previous routines are no longer working. Lunchtime in particular is problematic as although there are enough tables and chairs, many of the children need some support with serving and feeding themselves. The nursery has always prided itself on having mealtimes that encouraged children to be independent, but now staff are finding that they are rushing children or doing things for them. They have decided to review their routines and re-think how they manage some day-to-day activities.

The team at Little Bees are right to re-visit their routines rather than to persist in something that it is not working for children or staff. Routines that work well can be disrupted by a change of numbers or a change in the age and needs of children even if additional staff are on hand. It may be that they will need to split the timings of lunch slightly so that fewer children are needing help at the same time.

Recognise the signs that children may need support

Experienced practitioners quickly spot the signs that children's responses are moving in the wrong direction. Shrieking voices may indicate that a game that started out quietly is about to become boisterous and potentially unsafe. A child who looks tired and sounds frustrated may not be ready to play a game requiring concentration and high levels of self-regulation. If you are working with several children, it is also worth observing overall what children's concentration and engagement levels are like. Once a few children are wandering, it becomes increasingly hard for this not to affect other children. As a result, quite quickly, the atmosphere in a setting can change. Being on top of this and then being proactive enough to introduce a new activity, organise a snack or put out new resources can make a significant difference.

Change the script

'Change the script' is a good technique to use when adults and children have fallen into a cycle of behaviour. The child stands on a chair at mealtimes; the adult tells them to get down. The child repeats the action; the adult repeats the words. If you repeatedly find yourself back in the same situation with the same child, you need to realise that your approach is not working! Changing the script requires doing something differently. It might be that a picnic is put outside and so the child cannot stand on the chair or that laminated photographs are put on the table for the children to look at. It can be helpful to talk to parents about the concept of 'changing the script' so that they can use it as a way of solving difficulties at home. It is very easy for adults to forget that their own responses and behaviours need to change in order to effect change in the child.

Case study

Darik is three years old. The childminder enjoys having him, but when he first arrives, he tends to pull out all the cushions from the settee and then goes on to tip out toys randomly. The childminder is aware that this is not a great start to the day because she needs to tell him to stop and then to encourage him to tidy up. Last night, the childminder phoned Darik's parents to let them know that she was going to take him straight to the park the next morning. When Darik arrived, the childminder was waiting and instead of going indoors, they went straight to the park. Darik had a good time and the childminder felt that this was a more positive start to their day.

This is a good example of the 'change the script' strategy in action. The childminder has changed the situation and as a result Darik is showing different responses. It may be that Darik had developed his own coping routine for leaving his parent. While the 'change the script' strategy will have broken the habit, it will be important for the childminder and the parent to create a new routine that works for Darik when they decide to start the morning at the childminder's.

Advantages and disadvantages of some commonly used strategies

We have considered some practical approaches that can be very helpful in creating a supportive environment for children to learn to be with others. In addition, it is also worth examining some other strategies that are commonly used with children.

Star charts and reward systems

Star charts or variants such as marbles in the jar are designed to modify behaviour over a period of time. The idea of a star chart is that children gain points, stickers or marbles every time they show a wanted behaviour. Once a child has collected a pre-determined number, they gain a reward.

UNDERSTANDING THE REINFORCEMENT MODEL

It is worth understanding how reward charts work in order to best use them with children who are developmentally ready. Reward charts are secondary reinforcers. They work a little like money in the adult world. A coin or a bank note in itself does not meet any particular need. It is a secondary reinforcer; you cannot eat it, play with it or drink it. Having said this, we learn to associate money with pleasure. This is because we learn that money can be used to acquire a primary reinforcer, something that will give us pleasure. Money can be exchanged for a meal, a trip to the cinema or those new shoes that you have been looking at. For children, the stickers that are put on the reward chart are secondary reinforcers. The primary reinforcer comes later when the reward chart has been finished.

HOW STAR CHARTS ARE USED IN THE ADULT WORLD

You may not realise it, but every time you sign up for a loyalty card, you are actually signing up for a star chart! Restaurant chains, supermarkets and airlines have all realised that they can influence adults' purchasing choices by rewarding them. Shoppers tend to prefer loyalty cards where they know that points are quickly converted into rewards. This is worth remembering when creating effective star charts for children.

HOW TO USE STAR CHARTS EFFECTIVELY

If you decide that a child may benefit from a star chart, here are some tips to consider:

Specific and realistic behaviours
Star chart systems work best when the behaviour that is to be rewarded is very specific and can become habitual. Behaviours also need to be realistic for the individual child. Hanging up a coat properly or remembering to wash and dry hands before eating are examples of behaviours that can be positively reinforced using a star chart. It is important to explain to the child why the skill or social behaviour is needed. Star charts that involve 'being good' or 'playing nicely' tend not to work because they are non-specific and children may not understand what exactly they need to do.

Age and stage
One of the main reasons why star charts may fail to change behaviour is that they are being used with children who are not developmentally ready to understand how they work. Secondary reinforcers, such as money or star charts, require that a child has sufficient cognitive understanding of the process. If children are under four years, it is unlikely that star charts will be an effective method to use. Older children who have difficulty in self-regulating or have low levels of language may find star chart-type methods frustrating.

Achievable

It is important to think about the number of stars, stickers or marbles that the child has to collect in order to gain the reward. It is always better if the number is relatively low to start with so that children can see that it is worth the effort of doing the 'desired' behaviour. If you are introducing a star chart for the first time, it can be worth ensuring that the child can achieve the reward by the end of the first session. Afterwards, you can lengthen the time it will take, but do always remember to make it achievable otherwise children will give up.

Avoid a large reward

It is important to think about the reward that the child will have when the star chart is completed. It needs to be something that the child will be interested in, but avoid choosing a reward that is very significant. This is because at some point, we need the child to move on beyond the star chart. If the focus is only on the star chart, the danger is that children may not start to enjoy showing the skill or behaviour for its own sake.

Reminding children

One of our roles is always to help children achieve the star chart. This might mean reminding them to wash their hands or to wait their turn on the slide. Children are always more likely to gain a social behaviour or skill if they feel successful. Our job is to help them be successful.

Don't remove an earned star or token

Some parents and adults make the mistake of removing the star, sticker or marble if the child shows unwanted behaviour. This can backfire as children become very angry and may go on to show further unwanted behaviour. This is understandable – if a supermarket took away some of your loyalty points because you bought an item in a rival supermarket, you would no doubt be furious. If tokens are repeatedly taken away, sometimes children protest by no longer taking an interest in the chart.

Q

We are a preschool with children aged 2–4 years. We are thinking of introducing star charts to help with toilet training with our two-year-olds. What are your thoughts?

While it is not uncommon to find parents and preschools using star charts with children for toileting, I am personally not a great fan. Toileting is not really about 'good' behaviour. Instead it is a physical skill that children can only acquire when the bladder is sufficiently mature. Turning toileting into a behaviour issue can be confusing for children and may actually cause them to become stressed. When children become anxious during toileting, there is a higher likelihood of other problems. These might include constipation or children physically becoming so tense that they cannot release the urine. Having said that, for older children who forget to go to the toilet before going outdoors or who don't wash their hands properly, star charts can be very useful. This is because, firstly they have the physical capacity to be successful and secondly, because we want to reinforce a good habit. A star chart may give children an added incentive and so might be useful in this case.

A

Time out

Time out or the 'naughty' step is often used by parents as a tool to manage their children's behaviour. It is also used in some settings. The reasons why adults use it and also how they implement it can vary immensely. This means that it has become quite a controversial tool.

WHEN AND WHO IT WORKS WELL FOR

Time out was originally devised for older children and teenagers. The aim was to create a safe space for them to calm down and reflect on their actions; it was not a means of punishing a child. It is a great tool in the right circumstances as children can learn the skill of distancing themselves from a source of anger or conflict. Stepping back as a way of managing anger is a great skill for children to learn and can help with self-regulation. Indeed, some children may even learn to choose time out independently when they recognise that their emotions are strong or they are not coping in a situation. Time out is also meant to be collaborative. Adults can talk to the child about their feelings in this space and check on whether or not the child is ready to re-join the other children. Time out works well when adults understand its true purpose and are not using it as a punishment or a way to temporarily isolate a child.

WHEN TIME OUT DOESN'T WORK

While time out can work well with some children, it is worth reflecting on when and who it might not work with.

Children with low levels of language
Time out rarely works with children with low levels of language and so is not a good idea for toddlers, two-year-olds or any children with a language delay. This is because typically they are impulsive and find it hard to 'think'. Thinking requires high levels of language and so is not available to them. As many of the behaviours that result in an adult deciding to impose time out are often unplanned and developmentally linked, some children may not always make the connection between their action and then being isolated. There is also the danger that when young children are made to do time out, they feel rejected by adults and so become distressed. This can then result in children becoming clingy or showing more attention-seeking behaviours.

Time out as a threat or punishment
When time out is used as a threat or a punishment, children start to resent it. This is a shame because the skill of self-exclusion is an important one and if children have negative feelings towards time out, they may not learn how to use it beneficially. In addition, there is a danger in the home environment, where time out occurs in the child's bedroom, that the child learns to associate this room with being unhappy. This can cause problems with learning to fall asleep.

Inappropriate time

One of the ways in which time out has been used inappropriately is that adults often pose a time limit on how long a child must remain isolated. For younger children who may not make the connection between the unwanted behaviour and being sent to the 'naughty step', sitting still can be impossible. This can lead to children then being reprimanded for not staying on the 'naughty step' or children who become so frustrated that they throw objects around.

HOW TO USE TIME OUT

Time out works best when adults are not using it as punishment, but as a tool to help the child. As we have seen, children need to have a good level of language so that they can use the time spent in time out to learn to calm down and reflect.

Saying sorry

One of the issues that is often a source of debate between adults is whether or not children should automatically be required to say 'sorry'. A good starting point when looking at this topic is to remind ourselves what the purpose of an apology is.

WHAT IS 'SORRY' FOR?

Sorry is usually a way of asking for forgiveness from another that we have hurt, physically or emotionally in some way. When saying 'sorry' works well, it is a good way for the victim's feelings to be acknowledged and a way of both sides moving on. For it to work as a tool to restore harmony, the child or person who is at fault needs to understand how their action has affected the other person and they need to be sincere in their apology. The child or adult who has been 'harmed' also needs to accept the apology. Learning when and how to apologise is an important social skill that children do need to learn.

DIFFICULTIES IN TEACHING CHILDREN TO USE 'SORRY'

There are some pitfalls when it comes to teaching children the skill of saying 'sorry'. It is worth being aware of these especially if you are deciding on a behaviour policy in your setting.

Saying sorry to avoid responsibility

Making children say sorry before they really understand what it means can backfire. It means that some children learn to say 'sorry' without any feeling or sincerity. This leads to children using it like a 'get out of jail card'. They say 'sorry' in passing to a child that they have hurt and then tell the adult that it is okay because 'I did say sorry'. Once children have developed this habit, it is quite difficult to help them learn to use sorry with feeling.

Directing the apology at the adult

The other drawback with insisting on children saying 'sorry' too early is that quite often they say 'sorry' to the adult rather than to the child that has been affected. They do this either because the adult is insisting on it or because they have learnt that saying 'sorry' to the adult will avoid any further consequences. In addition, where adults force a 'sorry' out of a child, it is likely that it will be said begrudgingly. This can result in the comical situation where the adult insists on the child repeating it again 'properly'. When this happens, the child can then become angry and start to resent the 'victim'.

HELPING CHILDREN LEARN HOW TO USE 'SORRY'

There are several ways in which we can help children learn about apologising.

Role modelling

One of the ways in which children can learn how to use sorry is if adults role model it appropriately. When we use sorry with children, it is important that our face matches up with the word and that we also make eye contact with the child. It is also helpful if we explain why we are using the word: 'I am so sorry because I stepped on your toe. It could have hurt you. I am sorry.' It is important that we role model apologising even when an act is inadvertent. This is because we have to help children learn that even if they did not intend to harm another child or adult, we should always say 'sorry' because of the net result.

Building on children's concern

From a fairly young age, children can show concern for others. We may see a child looking worried when another child cries or is hurt. When a child has caused another to cry, it is important to notice whether or not the child looks concerned. If so, this is a good sign and we need to build upon it. We can say something such as 'You did hurt Jake, but he will feel better soon. It is not a nice feeling to see others upset, is it?'

Making amends

Making amends is a concrete way of saying sorry and can be a first step in children learning about apologising. A two-year-old can be encouraged to give the other child an object such as a toy or resource. Showing 'sorry' is often a better first step than saying 'sorry' as it helps children to take a little more responsibility for their actions. Making amends can also be used with children who are using 'sorry' as a passport to escape responsibility for their actions.

Puppets and storytelling

With children who have good levels and language and can relate to stories, using puppets and storytelling can be helpful. You can create stories where there is a 'perpetrator' and a 'victim'. You can have different scenarios including ones where the perpetrator refuses to say sorry. Using stories and puppets, you can encourage discussion about when and why 'sorry' should be used.

Q

What should we do if the child who has been hurt does not want to accept an apology?

As we have seen, saying 'sorry' is a reciprocal action and for it to work, it does require the other child to accept it. It is totally within a victim's right to refuse a 'sorry'. It may be that the child is still feeling angry or upset. If this is the case, it is worth leaving things until both parties have calmed down. Insisting on an apology can cause further problems as the 'victim' can learn to get attention by remaining upset. It is also worth explaining to the child who caused the problem that sometimes you have to wait before you can apologise.

A

Q

We don't insist that children should say 'sorry', but some parents and even staff have queried this.

I would start by finding out what the objection is. Sometimes people feel that if a child has not said 'sorry', that the child will 'get away' with the action and so will repeat it in the future. If this is the case, it is worth reassuring parents or staff members that if an action is deliberate, the child will always be reprimanded in some way. It is also worth explaining that saying 'sorry' will not necessarily stop a child from repeating a behaviour. Indeed, many children come to the conclusion that they can do what they want, provided they say sorry afterwards.

A

Q

We are developing a behaviour policy. At what age is it appropriate to expect children to say sorry?

This is a difficult question to answer because as we have seen children need certain developmental skills in order to apologise effectively. Rather than have a blanket rule about saying sorry, instead consider having a case-by-case policy according to the child's level of understanding.

A

Stickers

Some settings agonise about whether they should give children stickers. It is one of those issues that can be controversial and so is worth examining. Firstly, we need to understand the purpose of a sticker. A sticker is a tangible and concrete reward. It is a primary reinforcer (page 15) as well as a visible reminder to a child that they have done something that has met with an adult's approval. For most children, stickers are a powerful reinforcement and are often used by parents as well as in settings. So far, so good, but there are arguments against using stickers which are worth being aware of.

EFFECTS ON OTHER CHILDREN AND PARENTS

Some settings find that when one or two children are singled out for stickers, other children become upset and there can even be complaints from parents. This is particularly an issue when children become older and stickers are a badge of honour.

HOW TO USE STICKERS

As a pragmatist, my personal take on stickers is that they are a useful tool, but need to be used carefully. Firstly, I would always consider whether a sticker is strictly necessary. Sometimes a smile, some praise or a thumbs-up will be just as effective. Sometimes, the promise of a sticker may be a great incentive as it removes a little tension from the family home or prompts children to get into the habit of something in a setting. In group settings or where there are siblings in a family home, I would make it transparently clear how to get a sticker and perhaps even venture more than one way, i.e. a sticker for tidying up or for remembering to wash hands.

Chapter 5

Practical ways to support children's behaviour

Every practitioner and parent will have times when they are not sure how to respond to a child or what is prompting a child's response. In this section, we look at how to be a 'behaviour detective' and a strategy for looking for patterns in children's responses. The majority of this section, however, is an A–Z of children's behaviours and responses with some suggested reasons for each as well as some advice on how to support the child.

Being a behaviour detective

A good approach when trying to work out how best to deal with a behaviour is to spend some time thinking about the reasons why it may be occurring. In some ways, it is like being a detective and methodically going through a list of questions to work out what the probable cause is. When I am asked about a child, I tend to go through the following questions in the order in which they are given here:

Most two-year-olds will find it hard to sustain cooperative play

1. How old is the child?

The starting point usually needs to be the age of the child or stage if the child's development is atypical. If behaviours are age or stage related, they need to be accepted as such and little or no fuss should be made. Instead, adults may need to adapt the environment and their working style and be ready to use strategies such as distraction.

2. How is their language developing?

Some behaviours are linked to children's level of language. Social behaviours that require children to self-regulate, wait and think about others require high levels of language. This is because language and impulse control are linked. If children have lower levels of language, the main focus of work will need to be about boosting children's ability to communicate. (See page 50 for information about typical language development.)

3. Are they tired?

When children become tired, self-regulation becomes harder. It may be that lack of sleep or being tired are affecting the children. A tell-tale sign that the trigger is tiredness is whether the child is able to cope with social situations and self-regulate according to their age and stage at other times.

4. Are they settled, sociable and happy?

Some behaviours that children show are linked to separation anxiety and feelings of discomfort. It is important to be objective about whether a child has a strong relationship with their key person. If this is not the case, thought might need to be given as to how to develop it further. From around three years, most children also enjoy playing cooperatively with other children. If children are not starting to take an interest and join others in play, this needs to be investigated further.

5. How is the child's home life?

Changes to children's home circumstances can affect how they interact with others in a setting. Children may show signs of anger but also attention seeking. Sometimes behaviours such as swearing and being aggressive can be linked to a child's interactions with siblings or older children out of the setting.

6. Could it be hearing loss?

Some children who have hearing loss can appear not to listen or may become very frustrated and aggressive with others. Glue ear can be particularly hard to pick up as hearing loss may be intermittent. (See page 52.)

7. Could the child be showing signs of abuse?

Some changes and types of behaviour may be signs that a child has or is being abused. While this may be an uncomfortable thought, it is important that it is still considered.

8. What is the child getting out of the current situation?

Children's behaviour is rarely planned and in some cases is not even conscious. Most children will repeat behaviour because it has become their way of expressing frustration, getting attention or something else. A good example of this is when a child whines or sulks in order to get an adult to change their mind. Working out what the child achieves by their behaviour can therefore give us a clue about how to deal with it. In some cases, such as attention seeking, it may be that the child needs to be given more time and attention in general (see pages 82-4).

Q

We have a child who deliberately throws chairs or toys around to seek our attention. We know this by the way that he looks at us first before doing something. We think that this is planned ahead.

This child has learnt how to gain your attention and by the sounds of it is very effective in doing so! Having said this, it is unlikely that the child planned when and how he would gain your attention the night before. In a different situation, you may find that his response is not the same. This is why children on outings often have great days. Have a look on page 83 to consider how to respond to this child's attention seeking.

A

Looking for patterns

As part of being a behaviour detective, it can be useful to look for patterns in children's behaviour. One of the ways of doing this is using a frequency or event sample. A frequency or event sample is a very simple way of tracking and logging incidents. It is a good starting point where a behaviour is frequent and you need to find out more.

CREATING A FREQUENCY OR EVENT SAMPLE

There are not set formats for a frequency or event sample and you will need to create one for yourself. A basic format would simply be the date and time of an incident along with a description of what happened.

Example of a basic event sample

Date: 18th July		Name of child: Annie
Number of events	Time	What happened?
1.	10.24	Refused to put on coat and threw it to the floor. Tried to hit adult.
2.	11.30	Poured drink on floor to gain attention.
3.	16.28	Attempted to bite adult when adult was with another child.
4.	17.04	Hit out at adult when it was time to tidy away toys.

GAINING MORE INFORMATION

The simple format can be useful especially for parents to record incidents, but in a setting, more information is needed:

- **What had happened prior to the incident?**
- **Where did the incident happen?**
- **Were other children present?**
- **Which adult responded?**

Date: 18th July			Name of child: Josie			
Number of events	Time	Prior to incident	Location	Other children present	Incident	Adult response
1.	10.24	Josie and Annie rushed to role play. Both wanted to put on fairy dress.	Indoors. Role play	Annie	Annie had started to put on the dress when Josie bit her on the arm.	Jason responded. Moved Josie to another activity.
2.	11.30	Josie was putting sand in a bucket.	Sand tray	Annie	Annie took the bucket and emptied it. Josie took Annie's hand and bit it.	Sarah responded. Took Josie over to book area to calm down.

USING THE INFORMATION

The information gained from a frequency or event sample can help us to understand what is happening more clearly. It may be that parents think that their child is 'always' having a tantrum when the reality is that the child has far fewer than they realise. Information from a frequency or event sample in a setting may also show that incidents only occur when particular children are around or only at certain times.

Once you have decided on a strategy, frequency or event samples can then be used to see whether the number of incidents is starting to diminish. This is important because sometimes adults do not always see how much progress a child is making, especially if there have been a few setbacks on one day.

USING A FREQUENCY OR EVENT SAMPLE WITH PARENTS

Frequency or event samples can be useful to share with parents. It can be a way of helping them see how strategies, if applied consistently, can really make a difference. A good example of this is using a frequency or event sample to help children stay in bed at night. It may be that on the first night, parents return their child back to bed 30 times, but on the second this falls to 20. It may still seem like a lot, but parents can see that progress is being made.

Case study

Keira is three years old. She is a happy child although very determined. When she sees something that she wants to do or when she does not want to do something, she tends to have a tantrum. Her tantrums can last for more than 20 minutes. Many of her tantrums occur at home, but she can also have them at her childminder's. To end a tantrum quickly, her parents tend to let her have what she wants although they do realise that this may be reinforcing her behaviour. Her childminder and her parents have ruled out any developmental reasons for these tantrums and have concluded that they have become a habit. Together, they have decided to use an event sample to see if there are any obvious patterns.

It is not uncommon for some children to use tantrums as a way of showing displeasure or to persuade adults to change their minds. Tantrums can be linked to lower levels of self-regulation. An event sample may be useful as a way of seeing if there is any pattern to them. Once a strategy to deal with Keira's tantrums is in place, it may also be useful to carry out another event sample to track progress. It is likely to take a little while before the tantrums will disappear and, in this time, it can be helpful for the adults to see that, day-by-day, the new strategy is making an impact.

An A–Z of behaviours

Childhood is symbolised by learning, joy and exploration. It is also a time when children learn how to negotiate and balance their needs with that of others. It is not surprising therefore that during children's earliest years, there will be times when they do or show behaviours that prompt adults to intervene. In this section, we look at specific behaviours and responses that may present themselves, along with strategies that might be effective.

Afraid of getting dirty/ sensory activities

Some children become anxious and refuse to join in some sensory activities such as painting, gloop games or playing in a mud kitchen.

Why some children may not join in with sensory activities

There are a few reasons why children may not want to play with sensory activities.

UNCOMFORTABLE SENSATION

Some children find the sensation of touching something sticky or grainy very uncomfortable and even distressing. This is linked to the way in which the brain handles information. The nerve endings in the hand send signals to the brain. In some cases, the brain interprets the information incorrectly as a threat, resulting in a 'flight' response. This instinctive response is similar to the way that you automatically take your hands away if you think that something will burn you.

CLOTHES

Some children are either told or feel that they cannot get their clothes dirty. Even when wearing an apron, they may still be concerned that they will get wet or dirty.

How to respond

It is important not to make a big deal when a child does not want to play with sensory materials. Indeed, forcing a child to get involved or bribing them with a reward is likely to backfire. When children are apprehensive, they are more likely to 'feel' things more acutely and so become more anxious.

TAKE OFF THE PRESSURE

To encourage children to engage with sensory activities, it is important to find ways of removing pressure from them. This might include not standing near the activity so that children can join in for as long or as little as they wish without feeling that they are being watched. It may also be useful to put out a bowl of water and a cloth so that they know that they can wash their hands whenever they want. For children who are concerned about their clothing, it is worth providing a choice of aprons or overalls.

LISTEN TO CHILDREN

For children with good levels of language, it can be helpful to hear why they find the materials or play uncomfortable. You can also ask children what would make using the materials easier for them.

Not all children find sensory activities comfortable

Afraid of getting dirty

REDUCE THE SENSORY IMPACT

Another strategy that can help children is to remove the sensory impact of the materials. This might mean wrapping dough in cling film or putting it in a clear freezer bag. This allows the child to handle it but with reduced feeling. Similarly, some children may prefer to wear plastic gloves to touch paint or gloop. Reducing the sensory impact of the materials can be a great first step for children as it helps to lessen anxiety but also habituates the hands to the materials. Over time, some children will be able to dispense with the gloves or wrapping.

ACKNOWLEDGE CHILDREN'S RELUCTANCE

It is important that children are not made to feel that they have 'failed' if they don't want to use or join in with some sensory activities. It can be worth saying something such as 'I can see that you are not interested in this, at the moment. That's fine'. This approach leaves the door open for children to have a go later on or on another day. It can also be helpful to make comments such as 'some children don't like sticky things on their hands, but then they get used to it'. This is useful as a way of helping them feel that their reaction is normal and not a problem.

Talking to parents

It is useful to gain parents' perspective on their child's reluctance to use sensory materials or to do anything that may make them dirty. In some cases, we may find that parents do not find it an issue especially if this type of play is not part of their tradition. Some parents may also have asked their child not to participate in activities that might make them dirty because they do not want their clothes spoilt. By understanding the parents' perspectives, we may be able to find a way forward of helping them to understand the value of this type of play and the social benefits that it brings. We may also need to find a solution to parents' concerns. In some cases, this might mean providing additional protective clothing for a child or explaining in more detail the learning potential within activities.

In some cases, we may find that parents report that their child has always had an aversion to certain sensations, in which case we can share some of the strategies that we have already considered.

Aggression

Aggressive behaviours include hitting, thumping and pushing others. Aggression in young children is not uncommon, but in some it can develop into a habit.

Why some children show aggression

From time to time, most children will be aggressive with one another. The aggression is temporary and is more burst-like. For some children, however, aggression may be a feature of how they interact with others and so they may need more careful interventions.

AGE AND STAGE OF DEVELOPMENT

As with other aspects of behaviour, children's age and stage of development is linked to how they behave with others. Young children have lower levels of self-regulation and language and so are more likely to find controlling their emotions difficult. They are also likely to be more impulsive and so may hurt another child without thinking about the consequences.

LANGUAGE LEVEL

The level of children's language is likely to affect how well they can manage their emotions. Where older children have lower levels of language, it is likely that they will show more aggressive behaviours. This is because they cannot negotiate or squabble with other children and so are more likely to hit out in some way. Recognising the role of language in helping children cope in social situations is essential.

SUSTAINED FEELINGS OF ANGER AND FRUSTRATION

For some children, aggression is linked to sustained levels of anger and frustration. There may be deeper emotional issues at play and so, alongside managing the behaviour, it will be important to work out the cause of it.

Changes in family circumstances are often a cause of angry behaviours and they may include the arrival of a sibling or step siblings, separation of parents, moving home or losing a significant adult in their lives.

IMITATING THE BEHAVIOUR OF OTHERS

Some aggression may be linked to what children have seen or experienced. It may be that there is an aggressive adult or older sibling in the child's life or they have witnessed domestic violence. In some cases, children may have been exposed to violent scenes in a computer game or film.

POWER

Some children learn that if they are aggressive, other children may give in to them. This can lead some children to feel powerful and so reinforce the behaviour. The act of aggression in itself may also make the child feel good.

ADULT ATTENTION

Some children, especially younger ones, may show aggressive behaviours in order to gain immediate adult attention. A tell-tale sign that the purpose of the behaviour is to gain adult attention is that the child is likely to pause and check first that an adult is watching.

How to respond when a child is aggressive

How you should respond to a child who has been aggressive will very much depend on what exactly has happened and the reasons behind it. The starting point, however, is always to remain quiet and calm. This can help to diffuse the situation. It can be worth checking out the other child and not necessarily saying anything straight away to the child who has shown the aggression. This has the advantage of allowing the child to calm down and also prevents children from learning that they will get immediate adult attention if they are aggressive towards others.

If the behaviour was a 'one off' and was likely to be age or stage related, doing anything more than reassuring the other child may not be necessary.

On the other hand, if this is an older child with good levels of language, it is worth sitting down with them and gently finding out more about what led up to the event as there may be more involved than first appeared, i.e. the child was being teased or not allowed to join in with the play. Talking through what happened can be helpful and ideally, you should encourage the child to think about how they could have managed the situation differently. You may also wish to consider whether an apology or an act of reconciliation is necessary.

Where children are frequently aggressive towards others, the priority is to prevent further incidences occurring, firstly to protect the other children, but also to help the child 'unlearn' the behaviour. To do this, you will need to keep the child alongside an adult when they are with or near other children for several sessions. You may also need to give them safer alternatives for them to express their anger and frustration.

Q

We have a child who often throws things when he is angry. Sometimes he throws things at us or children, while at other times, he throws things on the floor.

This sounds like a very frustrated and angry child. Your first step needs to be removing the other children and adults from the immediate vicinity. You should also quickly do a risk assessment to check that there are no objects around that if thrown could cause him harm. You might also watch out for objects and items that are valuable in some way. It is important to stay extremely calm and possibly silent as there is a danger that you could fuel his anger. In some ways, this level of anger and aggression is like a tantrum (see page 134). The good news is that children cannot sustain this level of anger for very long, but you will need to work out why he feels such anger and then work to resolve it.

A

Preventing aggressive behaviours

There is no single way to prevent children from showing aggression as it depends very much on the cause. Here are some strategies you can try:

BE PROACTIVE

It is very important to be proactive when children have been aggressive. It may mean being alongside them for periods of time, especially when they are tired or in situations where they are likely to become frustrated.

LANGUAGE LEVELS

If the child's aggression is linked to language levels, it is worth finding ways to help them communicate their needs. You may create some visual prompts for them but also work on increasing the amount of interaction that is available. It may also be necessary to talk to parents about a referral.

PROVIDE OPPORTUNITIES FOR EXPRESSING EMOTIONS

Some children can benefit from having 'legitimate' opportunities to express feelings of anger. Physical activities that allow children to throw or hit can work well, as can sensory activities such as painting, music and dough.

POSITIVELY ACKNOWLEDGE THE CHILD

Children who have been aggressive need plenty of positive attention and acknowledgement, especially when they have managed their feelings of disappointment or frustration more appropriately.

Talking to parents

It is important to talk to parents if a child is frequently showing aggression which is not age or stage related. Understanding the cause of aggression is key to knowing how best to deal with it. A good starting point might be to find out whether the parents have noticed any changes in behaviour or have noticed frustrated behaviours.

While sometimes aggression is simply a sign of tiredness or language delay, it may be that there has been an incident or change of circumstances at home, or the child has had a traumatic experience. This is sensitive territory and sometimes parents may become very defensive. As practitioners have a duty of care towards the child, you may need to consider whether there is a safeguarding issue and, if so, you should always pass on your concerns, however difficult this may seem at the time.

Some children need safe ways of expressing their anger or frustration.

Anxious or lacking in confidence

Some children can appear anxious and lacking in confidence. We may notice that they are reluctant to join in or often seek reassurance. They may become tearful over relatively minor things. Children who are very anxious or lacking in confidence may miss out on opportunities to learn or socialise with others. This means that it is important to find ways of supporting children in order that they can develop strategies and skills.

Why some children may be anxious or lacking in confidence

There are a number of reasons why children may appear to be anxious or lacking in confidence. It will be important to talk to parents about how they view their child at home.

TEMPERAMENT

Some children seem to be pre-disposed to anxiety when in unfamiliar situations or where routines have to be changed. Parents will often have noticed early on in their children's lives that they have often seemed unsure.

ATTACHMENT

Some children may show signs of anxiety or lack in confidence because they have not formed a sufficient bond with an adult in the setting. With young children, a strong attachment to another adult is needed if parents are not present in order that they have a 'safe base'. Where children seem unsure and anxious, always start by considering whether they have a sufficiently strong attachment with at least one adult in the setting. A good sign that this attachment is in place includes a child being happy to see the adult and also seeking out physical contact.

EXPERIENCE

Some children can have an incident or experience that has made them become fearful or anxious. It will be important to talk to parents about anything in the child's history that might have been the trigger for anxiety.

LOW LEVELS OF SELF-EFFICACY

Self-efficacy is the ability to imagine oneself as being potentially competent. It is thought to begin in infancy if babies and young children are given opportunity to exercise some level of control in their lives. Where adults are overprotective and step in too quickly to help children in case they fail, children may not develop a sense of competence. In some cases, low self-efficacy can also occur because parents' expectations of their child are too high and the child is afraid of failing. (See also page 31, Self-identity and adults' expectations.)

How to respond

There are many different ways in which we can help children who are anxious or lacking in confidence.

AVOID RUSHING CHILDREN

Some children who are anxious or lacking in confidence cope better when they are not being rushed. Allowing plenty of time is often a good strategy as it allows children to gradually take stock of a situation.

AVOID PRESSURISING CHILDREN

It is also unhelpful for children to be pressurised into doing something that they are not quite ready for. In the same way, you should avoid making the child the centre of adults' and other children's attention. This can backfire, as children may dislike having attention drawn to them and therefore feel more anxious and stressed.

ROUTINES

Children who are feeling anxious can be helped by having some routines in place, particularly at the start of the session. Knowing what to expect can reduce stress and so help children to gain in confidence.

VISUAL TIMETABLES

Where transitions are difficult for children, it can be worth using visual timetables so that children know what to expect next.

EMPOWERMENT

The key word in supporting children who are anxious or lacking in confidence is 'empower'. Children need to feel and see for themselves that they can be competent or take some level of control and therefore grow in confidence. There are many ways of doing this. We might, for example, give a child some responsibility such as feeding the goldfish or counting up the scissors at the end of the session. We can also give children some small choices so that, little by little, they start to develop more confidence.

Talking to parents

It is helpful to find out from parents how they view their child. It may be that at home, they perceive the child as being confident or they may report that the child has always been slow to trust or to join in. If parents have noticed that their child is hesitant or more anxious than usual, it will be important to explore possible triggers with parents. Depending on the reasons behind the child's anxiety, it will also be helpful to agree with parents some strategies that you may jointly try out and then review.

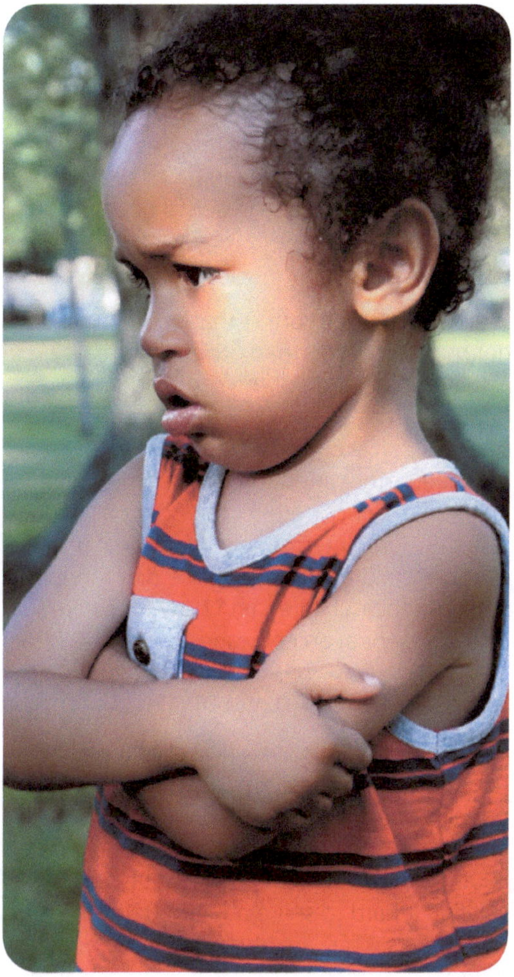

Attention seeking

Attention-seeking behaviours come in all guises – from the high-pitched scream of a toddler through to the carefully-timed tipping out books in a quiet area. The key feature of attention-seeking behaviours is that they are carried out to get the immediate and focused attention of an adult.

Why children may show attention-seeking behaviours

It is natural and perfectly healthy for children to seek the attention of adults. The attention of adults gives children reassurance, confidence and a sense of wellbeing. The amount of attention that children need can vary according to children's personality, as well as their age and stage of development. The problem with attention-seeking behaviours is that children learn to do things that are inappropriate to get an adult's attention. There are many reasons why children may get into the habit of showing unwanted behaviour in order to get attention.

PERSONALITY

While it may seem unfair that some children get more attention than others, the reality is that two children of the same age may need different amounts of attention. This is because some children are more extrovert and need more attention, while other children may be more independent and self-sufficient. Interestingly, parents of two or more children will report the differences between their children and how these are often present at an early age.

AGE AND STAGE OF DEVELOPMENT

The amount of attention that children will need not only varies from child to child but also according to age. Children under three years are likely to need significant adult attention and, particularly at two years, will find it hard to share adults' attention with others. They are also likely to be very demanding of adults. Once children reach three years or so, they are likely to need less adult attention as they start to be able to play with each other, although some children will still want to spend time close to adults.

INSUFFICIENT ATTENTION FROM ADULTS

For whatever reason, attention seeking has one particular cause – the child is not in receipt of sufficient attention and so has learnt strategies to gain immediate adult attention. In some cases, attention-seeking behaviours are prompted by a change in the family dynamics, e.g. a breakdown of the parents' relationship or the arrival of step siblings or a baby.

In other cases, parents may not be particularly aware of their child's need for positive attention and so may have fallen into the habit of only giving attention when the child is demanding of it through unwanted behaviour. Ironically, when children show attention-seeking behaviours, adults (including parents) are less likely to give children positive attention, and this in turn can prompt children to increasingly use attention-seeking behaviours.

CHANGES TO THE AMOUNT OF ADULT ATTENTION AVAILABLE

We may sometimes find that children who have a lot of attention at home can find it hard to adjust to being within a group and so develop attention-seeking strategies. In many ways, these children have been quite lucky, as language development is closely linked to the amount of attention that children have been shown. The good news is that these children are likely to quickly adapt to sharing attention, if they are given sufficient support.

TIREDNESS

Many children will show attention-seeking behaviours when they are tired because they cannot access the activities and resources independently or with other children. This is because being tired affects children's ability to concentrate and persevere.

STIMULATION

Some children resort to attention-seeking behaviours when they lack stimulation. This means that you should think carefully about the activities and resources that are available. Think about whether they are sufficiently interesting for the child and also a good fit for the child's current abilities and interests (see also page 89).

DIFFICULTIES IN BEING WITH OTHER CHILDREN

Some older children find it easier to be with adults than they do other children. There are several reasons for this. They may have mainly had adult company and not developed the strategies for being with other children or their play may be more developmentally sophisticated than that of the other children. Where attention seeking is a result of difficulties being with other children, it may be useful for adults to spend time role modelling play and also scaffolding interactions between the child and other children.

All children need and seek adult attention; this child has done so in a positive way

How to respond

There are two strands to responding to attention-seeking behaviours. It is important that they work in parallel.

STRAND 1 – DURING THE BEHAVIOUR

When the attention-seeking behaviour is taking place, it is important that absolutely no attention is given to the child. This means no eye contact, no turning towards the child and no talking to them! The aim is to imagine that the behaviour is simply not happening. It requires adults to be very single minded, as turning a head or telling a child to stop the behaviour is likely to be the more instinctive response. In some cases, you may also decide to move away from the child as attention-seeking behaviours are likely to continue where there is an audience. You can only do this if you feel that the child will be safe.

If the child is doing something that is potentially dangerous to themselves or to others, take away the item(s) or, as a last resort, remove the child from the area. It is important to stay completely calm and, again, not to interact or make eye contact with the child. If other children say something to you, just thank them for their concern and say that the child in question is just finding life a little difficult at present, but all will be well.

Once the behaviour has stopped, it is then important that the child receives positive attention. No reference to their attention-seeking behaviours is necessary. Indeed, talking about how they have behaved is likely to backfire. Getting plenty of positive attention is the second strand and needs to work alongside the strategy of avoiding giving the child attention during the attention-seeking behaviour.

STRAND 2 – PLENTY OF POSITIVE ATTENTION

As the attention-seeking behaviours are prompted by the child needing more attention, the second strand is designed to provide plenty of positive attention for the child. The aim of this approach is to lessen the need for the child to show attention-seeking behaviours. You should therefore aim consciously to look for opportunities to spend more time with the child. At first, this will need to be quite intensive, if you are to reduce the attention-seeking behaviours. Look out for activities where the child can come alongside you and you can give plenty of positive acknowledgement. If you have tracked when attention-seeking behaviours are more likely to occur (see page 82), you can use this information to help you increase the amount of positive attention that the child receives during these critical times. Providing positive attention requires a proactive approach; this means providing attention before the child has had a chance of showing any attention-seeking behaviours. It may take a while to 'reboot' the child's understanding of how to gain adult attention, so expect to be proactive in providing attention for at least a couple of weeks. Once the child is showing more appropriate ways of gaining your attention, you can start to reduce the intensity of positive attention. Having said that, for some children, increased levels of attention will need to continue if the underlying triggers such as family circumstances remain unresolved.

While it may seem time consuming to provide high levels of positive attention, it is worth it in the long run. If positive attention is not freely given, children tend to increasingly show more extreme ways of gaining adult attention.

Q

We have a child who seems to need a lot of attention. It does not seem fair that some children demand and then get more attention than others.

As we have seen, there are many reasons why some children will need more attention. Whatever the reason, it is important that adults proactively give them the attention they need. This avoids them learning to gain attention inappropriately. Interestingly, it takes less time to give a child a little attention than it does to sort out a situation when a child has sought the attention. Over time, when a child is feeling more secure, you can start to encourage a child to become more independent.

A

Talking to parents

Attention-seeking behaviours are not unusual and so it is worth letting parents know this when talking with them. It is worth seeing whether the same type of behaviours occur at home. In some cases, attention-seeking behaviours can be situation specific and so parents may not report any difficulties at home. Where parents also report that their child seeks attention inappropriately, it is worth sharing with them the strategy of ignoring attention-seeking behaviours while radically increasing the amount of positive attention the child is given. For some parents, it may be helpful if you suggest ways in which positive attention might be given, e.g. talking to a child while getting dressed or at mealtimes. It may also be worth suggesting that there are times when there are no televisions, tablets or phones around, so that undivided attention can be given. As some attention-seeking behaviours such as interrupting adults or having temper tantrums may have become well established, it can also be worth asking parents to keep a diary. This can help them to see that over time the frequency of the attention-seeking behaviours is reducing in response to the child having more positive attention from parents.

Biting

Biting can be a frequent problem in group care settings. Children who start to bite are likely to bite again unless steps are taken to prevent it. Some children who start biting may get into the habit of repeatedly biting the same child. This naturally makes parents very distressed.

Why children may bite

There are several reasons why children may start to bite or keep on biting.

AGE AND STAGE OF DEVELOPMENT

Biting is not uncommon between the ages of 18 months up until three years, although it is likely to occur amongst children just after they have turned two years. If children continue to bite beyond the age of three or four, it may be that there are deeper underlying issues that need to be resolved.

LANGUAGE LEVELS

One of the reasons why the majority of biting incidents occur between 18 months up until three years is because children typically do not have sufficient language to express their needs and to self-regulate their behaviour. This means that they become easily frustrated with other children. The link between language levels and biting means that some older children with language delay may show this behaviour.

EXPLORATORY

The mouth is a key way in which babies and young children explore. Typically, mouthing disappears by around 18 months, but for some children the need to put things in their mouth or to use their mouth to explore continues. This can sometimes be linked to learning or sensory processing difficulties. When older children bite, it is worth considering whether they use their mouth to explore at other times.

ATTENTION SEEKING

Some children learn to use biting or the threat of biting another child as a way of getting adults' attention. If this is the case, you will need to combine the strategies suggested for attention-seeking alongside those for biting (see page 82).

UNEQUAL RELATIONSHIPS

Some children may bite older children or siblings because they cannot express themselves and are not physically as strong. Some first bites occur because an older child or sibling teases a younger child.

CHANGES TO FAMILY CIRCUMSTANCES

Some children start biting when their family circumstances change. It may be the arrival of a new sibling or the change in relationship status of the parents. This can result in some pent-up frustration which then spills over in the setting.

LACK OF STIMULATION

While lack of stimulation does not in itself cause the biting to occur, it can create the conditions for a child to continue to bite. Most bites amongst two-year-olds occur when children are not engaged with an adult and are left to their own devices. As two-year-olds' social skills are still in development, this can create the condition for a bite to take place.

How to respond

Biting is one of those behaviours where you need to be very proactive. Biting can quickly become a default setting for a child and your aim should be to prevent another bite from occurring. Reprimanding the child will not prevent a further bite.

UNDERSTANDING THE POWER OF THE BITE

Biting seems to have a powerful effect on the child. The reinforcement gained from biting seems to be so strong that children find it hard not to bite again. This is perhaps because the mouth is designed for food and biting is part of eating. In addition to the sensory nature of the bite, the child will also gain an immediate reaction from the child that has been bitten and this can make the biter feel powerful. Biting also provokes an immediate and intense reaction from adults. This can cause some children to bite in order to gain adult attention.

BITING IS OFTEN SITUATIONAL

Interestingly, biting seems to be quite situational. A child who bites indoors may not bite outdoors. Indeed, most bites occur indoors. The situational nature of the bite means that parents may report that their child is fine at home and has never attempted to bite parents or siblings.

STEP 1 – DEALING WITH THE CHILD AT THE TIME OF A BITE

Start by going up toward the child, but avoid eye contact. Instead, look at the victim. Comfort the victim and ignore the biter. If possible, turn your back on the biter. This can prevent children from learning that biting gives immediate and undivided adult attention. It also sends out a clear message that their action was unwanted as a fuss is made of the victim.

Once the victim has been comforted, turn your attention to the biter. If the child is a younger child, move to step 2. If the child is older and is talking very well, you should calmly and quietly say something such as 'X is upset because you bit her. What can you do to make X feel better?' (See saying sorry, page 66). Then you should move to step 2.

STEP 2 – PROTECTING THE OTHER CHILDREN

The next step is to prevent another bite from occurring. Usually, once a bite has occurred, the likelihood of another bite occurring is high especially in the following hours. To prevent this from happening, you need to make sure that there is an adult engaging constantly with the child until the end of the session. This does not need to be one-to-one attention. The child can join in a group activity with an adult beside them or go over to play with others, but an adult must be with the child and actively engaging with them. Just supervising is not enough as a bite can occur very quickly. The aim is simple: you need to get to the end of the session without another bite occurring. Do not make any comment to the child about the bite or why such intense attention is being given. This is important because we do not want children to learn that if they bite, they can spend more time with adults.

STEP 3 – RE-INTEGRATION

It usually takes three bite-free days or sessions before it is safe for the child to be allowed freely to play or be with other children. Allow longer if the child has bitten many times before. It is wise to start off by allowing the child to be in a different room or space than where the bite occurred. Begin with 15 minutes and then build up gradually. As some biters target certain children, it is also helpful if the original victim is not near the (hopefully) now ex-biter. It is also worth not talking to the child about their past biting behaviour; simply keep a close eye on them.

It is worth keeping a close eye on children for a while after they have bitten

TALKING TO THE PARENTS OF THE CHILD WHO HAS BEEN BITTEN

You will need to explain how you intend to keep their child safe. This means explaining how you will not re-introduce the biter to the child until you are totally sure that this phase has passed.

Q

Some parents say that they have stopped their child from biting at home by biting them back. Is this advice to pass on?

NO! It is an offence for anyone, including parents, to bite a child. Parents need to know that they would be breaking the law and social services would become involved. It is always worth telling parents that this is the case whenever biting is ever mentioned. You should also let parents know that if they ever said that they have or would bite their child, you would be required to report this.

A

Talking to parents

Many parents will be upset if either their child has been bitten or has bitten another child. It is important to reassure parents of very young children that biting is developmentally normal. It is also worth explaining that biting is normally situational although do ask if there have been any bites at home. Talk to parents about whether lack of sleep could be exacerbating the situation.

For parents of older children, you will need to consider with them what underlying factors may be causing the biting. This may include rough play with siblings, teasing or changes to the family dynamics that have left the child feeling powerless or frustrated. It is also worth thinking about whether the child has a language delay or communication difficulty and, if so, organising a referral promptly.

Whether or not there is an underlying cause for a child's biting, the key strategy is prevention when the child is in the setting. While parents may wish to say something to the child, this is unlikely to help and may cause more problems. Ideally, they should not say anything to the child, but instead make sure that the child is getting plenty of positive adult attention at home and, if necessary, more sleep.

Concentration

It is not uncommon for practitioners to comment on children's lack of concentration. They may find that children are easily distracted or that they may not settle down to activities for very long.

Why children may not concentrate

Concentration is a part of a collection of skills involved in the brain taking in and storing information. This is known as information processing. Concentration is about focusing one's attention on a particular activity for a period of time. It also means 'tuning out' from other things that the brain automatically notices, e.g. background movements, noise and smell. There are many myths about concentration. It is said, wrongly, that children can only concentrate for one minute for each of their years. Thus, in theory a baby can only concentrate for a minute and a four-year-old can only concentrate for four minutes. This clearly does not stack up as during play many children will concentrate for quite long periods.

TIREDNESS

One of the main reasons why children may find it hard to concentrate is tiredness. Children who are not sleeping sufficiently are likely to find it hard to concentrate for long periods. In addition, being away from home and with other children is tiring for some. This means that as the session or day wears on, children are increasingly likely to find it hard to concentrate.

AGE AND STAGE OF DEVELOPMENT

There are differences in the way in which children can concentrate as they develop. These are linked to changes in the brain and

an overall greater capacity for information processing. Young children are likely to be more easily distracted and may concentrate for short bursts of time; for example, you may find that a two-year-old will leave an activity, but then shortly afterward return to it.

ACTIVITY LEVEL

Levels of concentration can also be linked to the levels of participation involved. Younger children find it easier to concentrate if they are physically active in some way. This is because the body can stay more alert when there is movement. Sitting still and listening requires more concentration than joining in mixing dough. (See also listening, page 100.)

SENSORY ACTIVITIES

Linked to activity level, children are likely to find it easier to concentrate if they participate in sensory activities such as playing with water, sand or dough. This is because the sensory materials stimulate the nerve endings of the hands and fingers, which in turn keeps the brain alert.

ADULT-DIRECTED ACTIVITIES

When activities are very structured and adult directed, concentration levels tend to be lower, especially in group situations. This is because children have to process information at the speed that it is being presented. In some cases, this might be slightly too much or too fast. Children can quickly become overwhelmed and so tune out. When children are playing or looking at something independently, they can go at their own speed. This is why children tend to concentrate for longer on child-initiated activities.

ANXIETY

Children who are anxious because they have not developed a strong key-person attachment in the setting may show lack of concentration. It is hard to concentrate when you are unhappy or looking at the door, waiting for someone to collect you.

LACK OF STIMULATION

Children are competent and hungry learners. As their skills develop, they become voracious in their appetite to try out new things and to develop things that they can already do further. Where children have been in a setting for many hours, the level of stimulation offered may no longer be sufficient. Toys and activities that helped children to concentrate when they were two or three years old may no longer provide enough challenge and possibilities for a four- or five-year-old.

TOO MUCH STIMULATION OR CHOICE

While lack of stimulation can be a problem, ironically too much stimulation can also cause problems for children. An environment with a lot of background noise or movement, or one that is very visually distracting can make it hard for children to focus, especially the very young. For some children, too much choice and possibility can also be the problem. This is likely to be the case with children who have not been in a large space before or who have not had many opportunities to play. This can mean that they become overwhelmed very quickly and so show very distracted behaviours.

DIFFERENCES BETWEEN INDIVIDUAL CHILDREN

As with all areas of development, there is a continuum of individual differences between children. Even in a very noisy and chaotic environment, some children are able to concentrate at length, while for others it is impossible.

HEARING AND EYESIGHT

It is always worth being aware that children's eyesight and hearing can affect their concentration. If children cannot see or hear clearly, it may be harder for them to concentrate. If you suspect that a child might not be hearing or seeing well, it is important to ask parents if they can seek a referral for a test.

How to respond

You cannot force children to concentrate. Instead, the focus needs to be on creating optimum conditions to support children.

TIMINGS AND NAPS

We know that tiredness is a key factor in children's ability to concentrate. It is worth thinking about doing activities that require high levels of concentration in those periods when children seem to be less tired. Many practitioners report that concentration levels are highest in the morning, but this will still depend on individual children.

ENVIRONMENT

Making changes to the environment can make a vast difference to some children. It is worth, during a session, getting down to a child's height and thinking about what children will be seeing and hearing. Think about the background noise and also visual distractions in the environment.

Smaller spaces

It can be helpful to create smaller spaces which are in some way screened off from each other. This means that children cannot be distracted by the passing movements of other children.

Reducing background noise

Make sure that all adults in the setting use quiet voices and do not call across the room. Think about putting in some soft furnishings and also mats and rugs to dampen down sounds. It can also be worth looking out for soundproofing foam which can be attached to screens.

Resources

For some children, the amount of resources on offer can be overwhelming for them. While having plenty of choice is the right thing for some children, for others it may be part of the problem. Some children may not be able to focus on a single activity while too many other possibilities are available. Think about creating some areas where resources are laid out in ways that help children see what they could do. This can be thought of as a play prompt. An example of this might be five or six cars with some cardboard tubes of different lengths, a few shoeboxes and some masking tape. While this prompts children to play with cars, they can experiment with the tubes and the shoe boxes, and some children may go on to create garages or tunnels. Other children may simply enjoy rolling the cars down the tube or just playing with the cars on a mat.

Feel-good resources

Many children concentrate for longer periods when sensory materials are available in sufficient quantities. This is because they feel good in the hands. Interestingly, the same is true of resources that are made from natural materials, e.g. wood, metal and fabric. Increasing the number of different sensory materials available for children can have a considerable impact on how children concentrate. It is also possible to combine sensory materials with toys, e.g. some real turf in a tray to go with a few farm animals or

Most children can concentrate for longer with sensory resources

a tray of bark chippings to go with some toy tractors. A good tip when buying resources and toys is always to put them in your hands and close your eyes. Chunky farm animals, for example, are played with for longer than skinny ones; equally, a beanbag feels better to throw than a light plastic ball. The 'feel factor' is particularly important when choosing resources for children aged between 18 months and three years.

CHALLENGE

For some children, lack of concentration is linked to lack of interest in what is available. This is often the case when children have spent hundreds of hours within a setting and so have run out of possibilities. It is worth planning carefully with this in mind. Think about what is new or different to make this activity or play opportunity 'fresh'. If children are with you for eight or ten hours, you may also need to put out different resources so that children can change how and what they play with.

THINKING ABOUT ADULT-DIRECTED ACTIVITIES

Adult-directed activities need to be carefully thought through. These are likely to be the activities that children find the hardest to concentrate on for any length of time. It is worth thinking about how you make these participative, varied and maybe also sensory. It is important to focus on individual children's information processing levels. Some children may need more repetition or time to master a skill or acquire a concept. Other children may need a faster pace, and going more slowly will mean that they 'turn off'. This is why group activities are so difficult to get right, as the variance between children might be significant.

SUPPORTING CHILDREN

Children who have not experienced many play opportunities or a large space may need an adult to be with them. The role of the adult will not be to direct the child but instead to act as a facilitator to make sure that the child can access the opportunity. A good example of this is completing a jigsaw puzzle: a child may start it and then be inclined to give up if a piece doesn't go in. An adult can suggest another piece or encourage the child to turn the piece. This way the child may finish the puzzle and gain feelings of success.

Q

We have several two-year-olds who are not good at concentrating. When they come in for the afternoon, they are often asleep in their pushchairs. Our policy is to wake them up so that they do not miss out. Is this the right thing to do?

Nap times are often important for young children as they help them to process information. Children who are woken up from a nap too early are likely to find it hard to concentrate. This means that they may not be able to access or learn from the play and opportunities that you have on offer. It is better for children to have a one hour nap and then have two hours of learning rather than be awake for three hours but gain very little.

A

Talking to parents

It is useful to talk to parents about their child's concentration levels. It may be that, at home, parents feel that their child is good at focusing on a game, toy or helping them with a task. In which case, it may be the environment in the setting that needs working on. Where parents can see that their child finds it difficult to concentrate, it may be that considering sleep patterns may be the first port of call (see page 38). It is also worth sharing with parents the strategies that we have considered earlier. If, together, there is a feeling that the child is showing unusually low levels of concentration, a referral should be sought.

Following instructions

There are times in every family and every setting when children do need to follow instructions. It may be as simple as putting on a coat because it is home time, or going to wash hands because they are dirty. Some children find it hard to follow instructions, and this can make adults very frustrated. Sometimes children may seem to forget, while at other times, the child may appear to ignore the instruction.

Following instructions is at times a necessity, but at the same time, we always need to remember that children are not mini-robots.

Why children may not follow instructions

There are many reasons why children may not follow instructions or do as they are told. Following instructions is linked to information processing skills, especially listening and concentrating. You may wish also to read these sections too (pages 88-91 and 100-103).

AGE AND STAGE OF DEVELOPMENT

Children's ability to listen to and follow instruction is age and stage related. Complex instructions with two or more parts to remember will be hard for young children to cope with. Instructions accompanied by gesture or showing what is expected will be easier. The chart shows typical stages involved with following instructions. It is worth noting that typical development would suggest that it is not until children are around four years old that they are able to follow instructions as part of a group.

Development of understanding and following instructions

Age	Following instructions
12–15 months	The child understands and follows simple instructions such as 'come here'.
15–18 months	The child understands a wide range of single words and some familiar phrases, e.g. 'coat on', 'give ball', 'cuddle teddy'. Child can give some named familiar objects to an adult.
18–24 months	The child can give a number of familiar objects on request. They can follow simple instructions without gestural cues, e.g. 'Where is your shoe?'
2–3 years	The child is beginning to understand familiar or routine phrases, e.g. 'Put teddy in the box'; 'Get your coat and bag'.
3–3 ½ years	The child understands sentences containing three to four key words, e.g. 'Put the big brick in teddy's bag'.
3 ½–4 years	The child understands sentences containing three to four key words, e.g. 'Put teddy in the big box', and questions or instructions with two parts, e.g. 'Get your coat and stand by the door'.
4–5 years	The child understands instructions given to a group of children and instructions containing sequencing words such as 'first', 'after' or 'last'.

MEMORY AND INFORMATION PROCESSING

Children's ability to listen to instructions and, more importantly, to remember them is very limited. This is because children's brains find it easier to process visual information, rather than information given to them orally. Children are more likely to remember an instruction where an adult has shown them what to do, rather than just talked about it. Children also take in information differently to adults. They may focus on things that are not relevant; a child who hears the adult say 'Do you see that brown door. Can you go and wait by that brown door?' may focus more on the 'brownness' of the door rather than on the 'stay'!

Timing and style

The gap between a child hearing an instruction and then following it out is critical. Children are less likely to remember an instruction which they cannot act on immediately. Children will also struggle if the instruction is very vague. The classic one which is very unhelpful is 'be good'!

Distraction and impulse control

Children will find it harder to follow instructions if there are other distractions that are more appealing. This means that they may start to put on their coat but then get waylaid because they see something more interesting. Children also have difficulties in managing temptation because they find it hard to regulate their impulses. Instructions that involve negatives, e.g. 'don't touch' or 'don't run', will be hard for children to stick to if there are temptations.

Divided attention

Young children will also find it hard to focus their attention on more than one thing (divided attention) and so, for example, they will find it hard to get dressed while watching a television or tidying up when talking to another child.

RELEVANCE

As we have seen from the age and stage chart, younger children may find it hard to follow instructions that are addressed to a group rather than to them individually. They may not realise that the instruction is for them!

Some older children may not follow instructions because they cannot see their relevance or the urgency. They may be happily involved in play and so do not see why they should stop.

ATTENTION SEEKING

Some children may not follow instructions in order to gain adult attention. If this is the case, this usually happens fairly immediately and the child may say 'no', or they may turn in the opposite direction.

HEARING

It is also worth considering whether children have a hearing loss. Not following instructions or seeming to have noticed what is happening around them can be a sign that a child has not heard. (See also page 100.)

How to respond when children do not follow instructions

There is no single way to respond when children do not follow instructions. It is not a good idea to raise your voice or to keep repeating them, especially if the child is ignoring them. If this happens, children can get in the habit of only responding on the third or fourth time of repetition. Instead, it can be worth physically approaching the child and gaining their attention. Then, once you have established eye contact, re-phrase the instruction using a firm but urgent tone. For children who are older and have good levels of language, you may wish also to explain the reason for the instruction and the consequences for the child. (See 'Terms and conditions', page 57.)

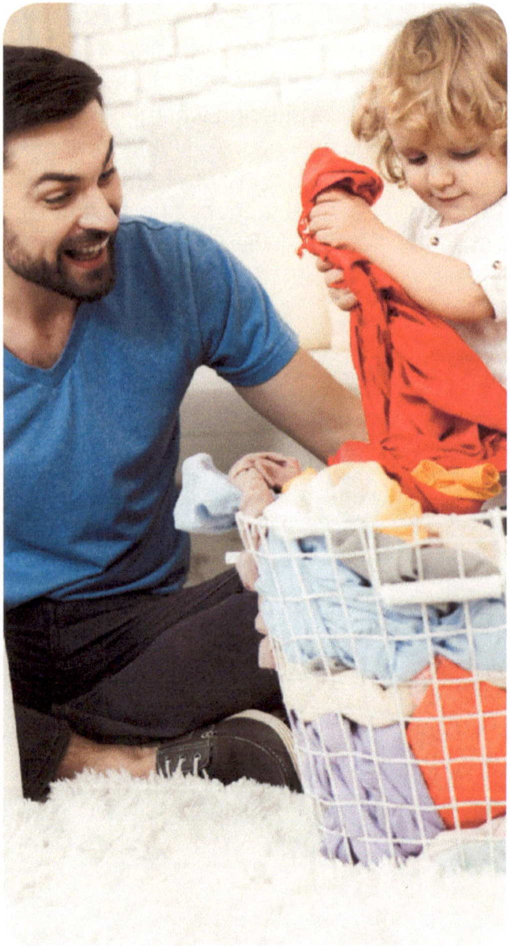

Helping children to follow instructions

FAIR EXPECTATIONS

It is essential to have fair expectations of children and to remember that what is important to an adult may not be that important to a young child. Children also are likely to be easily distracted and so forget what they are meant to be doing, especially if a lot of time has gone by since the original instruction. As we have seen, vague instructions are also very hard for children to understand and act upon. It is always worth referring to the age and stage chart to check that expectations are fair for children.

AT THE TIME AND REMINDERS

Children are more likely to follow instructions if they are able to act upon them immediately. This is linked to memory and concentration. Children may also need frequent reminders and encouragement.

KEEPING IT POSITIVE

It would appear that keeping instructions positive is more effective than telling children what not to do, e.g. 'wait' rather than 'don't move' or 'walk' rather than 'don't run'. Children are also more likely to remember an instruction if the adult is not stressed. This is because otherwise the child's focus becomes the adult's face rather than the words or actions.

SHOW, NOT TELL

As young children find words harder to process and remember than images, wherever you can, it is worth 'showing' an instruction. This might mean holding up a coat or pointing at the place where an object is to be put.

KEEPING IT SIMPLE AND SHORT

For younger children, it is worth leading them through a task with one instruction at a time. It is also worth keeping instructions short and to the point in order to help them focus on what is important, e.g. 'Walk. You need to walk.'

EXPLAINING THE RATIONALE

Older children find it easier to remember and keep to instructions if they can understand the rationale for them. This means explanation is a useful tool, especially where we can link it to other's feelings and needs, e.g. 'we need to be quiet because there are two children who are asleep'.

POSITIVE ENCOURAGEMENT AND PRAISE

It is important for children to gain positive encouragement when they have completed tasks or remembered how to act or behave. This helps them to feel successful and is more likely to make them feel capable.

Talking to parents

Parents can become very frustrated when their children do not follow instructions. It is worth helping them understand the age and stage implications, as well as strategies that can help children. It is also important for parents, especially if they are very busy, to think about the balance between giving instructions and providing quality time with their children. While all families need to sort out organisational issues such as going to bed or getting up in the morning on time, there also needs to be some time when children can simply 'be' with their parents without any demands.

Parents also need to understand that however much their child seems to be sensible, when it comes to safety issues, relying on a child to remember not to touch matches or to stay still while the car is being parked is risky. Children can easily be distracted and so may follow their impulses.

Children find it easier to follow instructions if they can see what they need to do

Interrupting

Some children constantly try to interrupt or disrupt adults as they are talking either to each other or to other children. Learning to wait for others and to recognise that they have needs is an important social skill which is also linked to turn taking and self-regulation.

Children find it hard not to interrupt others when they are excited

Why children may interrupt

There are many reasons why children may try to interrupt or disrupt conversations between others. Firstly, it is important to recognise that many adults interrupt each other as part of day-to-day conversations.

AGE AND STAGE OF DEVELOPMENT

Young children are likely to interrupt because they do not yet have the self-regulation skills needed to take turns or to realise that others have needs.

LANGUAGE LEVELS

Linked to age and stage are children's language levels. Children with low levels of language find it hard to wait their turn as they have a need to say what they think at the time.

EXCITEMENT

When children are excited by something, it can be hard for them to self-regulate and also keep their thoughts internal. If older children do not regularly interrupt, but do so when excited, it is important not to see it as a problem.

ATTENTION SEEKING

Older children who interrupt may be trying to seek attention. They may do this by tapping on an adult's back or even telling an adult to be quiet!

HABIT

Some older children may also interrupt because the adults that they are with don't mind or have not asked them to wait. This can be a habit.

How to respond

How you respond will depend on children's developmental and skill level.

YOUNG CHILDREN OR OLDER CHILDREN WITH LANGUAGE DELAY

For young children, it is worth saying something such as 'I know you are waiting', but without giving any eye contact. Not turning around or making eye contact can prevent young children who are naturally impulsive from learning to get attention this way. It can also be worth passing something to the waiting child as a way of helping them to wait.

OLDER CHILDREN

If interrupting has become a habit, it will be important not to respond immediately to the interruption. This means no immediate eye contact. We can then say aloud to the child that they will need to wait. Afterwards, we will need to explain to the child why we were unable to immediately respond to them.

How to prevent children from interrupting

We know that children find it hard to wait or take turns. While it is important for children to learn to wait a little, it is also important that we are fair to them. If we know that we will be tied up in a conversation or play with other children, we may need to tell an older child and give them a choice of either waiting nearby or telling them that we will come and find them when we have finished.

POSITIVELY ACKNOWLEDGING CHILDREN WHO WAIT

It is important to make a comment when children have waited, so that they can see that this is a valued skill. It is helpful also if children can be told the positive impact of their waiting, e.g. 'I saw that you were waiting patiently. Ayse needed to tell me something that was important for her.'

USING STORY AND PUPPETS

Stories and puppets can be useful to reinforce the importance of waiting one's turn. You could have a story where a character tries to tell someone about losing a toy, but every time they try to say something to the adult, another child comes along and interrupts them. Afterwards, we can ask children why it is important that everyone gets a chance to be listened to. We can also talk about in what circumstances it is fine to interrupt others, e.g. if there is an accident or if someone feels poorly.

ROLE MODELLING

It is important that adults, too, can show that they do not interrupt. If another adult is talking to a child, it would be good if the child can finish what they are saying before the adults start to talk. If this is not possible, it is important for children to hear an adult apologise for interrupting them.

Talking to parents

Assuming the child is old enough or has sufficient language to be able to regulate their impulses, we may need to talk to parents about how and when their child interrupts. It may be that in the home, this is not an issue or that the parents are unaware that their child has developed this habit. Some parents may be aware that their child is interrupting them, but their strategy may be to become cross and by doing so give their child immediate attention. It is worth working with parents to create a unified approach over a short period of time so that the child is able to develop self-regulation strategies. A good time for parents and you to work on this child's behaviour is at pick-up times as this is often a time when some children try to sabotage conversations.

Lining up

Some settings with older children find that difficulties occur when children are meant to be lining up. They may touch each other, try to be first or last and may not stand in a straight line.

Why children may find it hard to line up

Lining up is something that is hard for children to do, and it is important to recognise that mostly it is done for organisational reasons.

AGE AND STAGE OF DEVELOPMENT

Lining up is not really appropriate for children under three years as it requires high levels of self-regulation. There will be some three-year-olds who also find it difficult, especially if required to wait for some time. Some children who have developmental delay will also find it very difficult or even distressing, as they may not feel comfortable being in close proximity with other children.

LACK OF STIMULATION

One of the great problems with lining up when children are in single file is that they cannot cope with the lack of stimulation. Unless they are at the front, or stand out of line, they cannot see in front of them, nor can they easily talk to other children. In addition, most lining up involves not holding or touching anything. This lack of stimulation means that children become quickly bored and so problems can soon escalate. The lack of stimulation explains why children push to be at the front or linger to be at the back, as these are the best places to be if you have to line up.

Responding to children who are not lining up

When children are not lining up, unless it is an emergency, it is worth immediately changing your approach. You could sing a song with the children or allow them to stand next to a partner. If children are likely to be waiting for a while, you could also suggest that they sit down. You should then reflect on changing practice so that lining up either is curtailed or it is made more enjoyable for children.

These children are happy because they can still talk

Ways to reduce lining up and ensure that it is enjoyable

Some settings, even schools, have virtually no lining up apart from to practise for fire drills. They achieve this in a number of ways:

SMALL GROUPS

One way to reduce lining up is to organise moving between rooms or areas in small groups. This is the most effective way of working with children under four. Using the adult–child ratio, each adult is responsible for a few children and then takes them outdoors, to the hall or wherever. This approach means that children can continue to talk to each other and waiting time is reduced.

LINING UP IN TWOS OR THREES

Lining up in twos or even threes, if space allows, is much easier for children. Straightaway they can talk to other children and so for a short time, it can be more enjoyable.

ENTERTAIN, TEACH AND DISTRACT

If children have to line up, it is important that there is an adult available to stimulate the children. This might mean sharing rhymes, playing musical or counting games. As lining up is otherwise 'wasted' time in terms of children's learning, it is worth planning for it.

REDUCE WAITING TIMES

Adults are so often busy herding children that they do not realise just how long some children have been waiting. If lining up is the only solution, it is important to think about ways of cutting the waiting time. It may be that children can sit in groups; when they are ready to move, and only when everyone is prepared, do the groups move off.

Q

We have to get the children to line up to access the school hall which is across the playground. We have 26 children aged three and four and there are just the two of us at times. Any ideas?

Try to make sure that both of you are ready and the children are ready, e.g. coats on, before the call to line up. This will reduce the amount of waiting time for children. Sing a song using clapping hands if there is any waiting. Consider encouraging the children to be in pairs as well. This means that the number of rows is just 13. If walking in pairs isn't appropriate, then after row 13, aim for a slight pause so that the group is slightly divided. Try also to give the children a simple task as a way to get there, e.g. walking on tiptoes or putting their hands on their hips.

A

Talking to parents

This is a behaviour that is organisational in nature and so has no real implications for parents.

Listening

Many parents and practitioners complain that children do not listen to them. This is because children may be easily distracted or they may talk or make random comments when they are meant to be listening. As language is a complex area and is often linked to behaviour, you might wish to read this section alongside page 50.

Why children may not listen

There are many reasons why children may appear not to be listening. It is also important to distinguish between listening in a group situation and listening when directly spoken to.

HEARING

It is very common for children to have hearing difficulties in their early years. The most common type of hearing difficulty is caused by 'glue ear'. This can cause a fluctuating loss; at times a child may hear well but on other occasions may have very low levels of hearing. (See also page 52.)

AGE AND STAGE OF DEVELOPMENT

It is essential to keep an eye on typical development in relation to paying attention and listening, as many adults' expectations are out of kilter with expected development. This can mean that children are reprimanded for not listening, when developmentally it is not appropriate. The chart below shows the typical ages and stages for attention and listening. Note how for the first few years, children will be easily distracted and how children between two and three years will find it hard to listen when talk is not directed at them. This makes group times such as circle time hugely challenging, as they are developmentally inappropriate for most children.

Development of attention and listening skills in children

Age	Attention and listening
6–12 months	• The child locates the source of another's voice with accuracy. • The child can now focus on different sounds, e.g. telephone, door bell, clock. • The child is extremely distractible.
12–15 months	• The child focuses on music and singing, and enjoys sound-making toys or objects. • The child listens & responds to simple, routine instructions. • The child begins to concentrate on self-chosen activities, resisting interference from adults.
15–18 months	• The child listens and responds to simple information and instructions, e.g. 'Ben put your shoes on'; 'Aysha, give to Daddy'.
18–24 months	• The child can concentrate on an activity they have chosen but can't tolerate direction from an adult.
2–3 years	• The child is beginning to listen to talk with interest but is easily distracted. • The child will listen to talk addressed to themselves but finds it difficult if prompts are not provided, e.g. use of name, 'stop & listen'.
3–4 years	• The child stops to listen for directions from an adult but may need support to do this, e.g. adult uses hand to ear for 'listen'. • The child enjoys listening to stories.
4–5 years	• The child is able to move focus between tasks but may still need to stop activity to listen.

LISTENING AND TALKING

It is important to understand the link between talk and listening. Until around the age of five or so, many children will talk as they are listening. This may seem strange, but when children are listening well, they should be making connections and thinking about what has been said. This may result in a child making frequent comments such as 'I like sausages' in response to a conversation about what will be served for lunch or 'our dog is called Millie' in response to a story about a dog. Developmentally, when young children are thinking, their thoughts appear in spoken language. This is known as external speech. As adults, we are able to think 'in our heads' or internally. It is only when children's language is well developed that they are able to 'quietly' think when they make connections. The link between listening and talking means that some children who appear to be listening may just be sitting quietly and not actually retaining or thinking about what is being said. Some practitioners may try to ask children to put their hands up if they wish to say something, but this is unlikely to work with children under five years, because their thoughts and thinking is spontaneous.

LANGUAGE DELAY

We have seen that talking and listening are interrelated. While it is typical for children under five to call out or find it hard to listen without comment, older children who still call out or find it hard to listen may have a language delay. If this is the case, it will be important to address the cause of the language delay and if necessary ask parents to seek a referral to the speech and language team. In some areas, early years settings can make a referral on behalf of the child with parental permission. In other areas, parents will need to seek a referral via their GP.

PROCESSING LANGUAGE

For children under four years old whose language typically is not fluent, it is also important to understand that words in themselves can be hard for children to process. Children often need longer to make sense of what is being said to them, and it is important that what is said is appropriate to their developmental level. Children also tend to find listening easier when there is a visual accompaniment, which is why children often need to look at the pictures in a book when it is being read to them.

Listing

ATTACHMENT

Children may not always make eye contact or appear to pay attention and listen to adults that they are not familiar with or comfortable with. Indeed, some young children may actually turn away or pretend that the unknown adult is not there.

BACKGROUND NOISE

Background noise can impact significantly on children's ability to listen. For some children, background noise can make it hard to hear what is being said and so affect how easily they can process what is being said. Background noise can also make it hard for children to concentrate and, in some cases, can be a distraction. (See page 89.)

NOT INTERESTING

Unlike adults, who learn to pay attention and listen even when they are bored, young children do not yet have these advanced skills. Developmentally, children listen best to things that are of direct interest to them. This means that a story which is of interest to them and at the right language level will be easier for a child to listen to.

How to respond

When children are not listening, it is important to think about the environment and your style of communication.

ATTRACTING CHILDREN'S ATTENTION

With very young children, we actually need to attract their attention before we start talking. Where young children are very involved in an activity, it will be hard to gain their attention and it may be worth waiting. We can attract children's attention by gently touching their arm, saying their name and then waiting until we have eye contact.

KEEPING IT INTERESTING

Children will be more motivated to listen when what is being said is of interest to them. This is often where circle times fall down. What another child has done may not be of any interest, and because children are not allowed a right of reply, it can mean that they quickly turn off.

Gaining children's attention is an important strategy in helping them to listen

SIZE OF GROUP

The easiest way of helping children to listen in group situations is to think about group size. As we have seen, quite often children need to talk in order to listen until they are very competent in their language. It is worth keeping group sizes down to a minimum so that it does not matter if children talk or comment.

GETTING THE LANGUAGE LEVEL RIGHT

One of the reasons why it is hard for children to listen in large group situations is that it is hard for the adult to get their language level right for every child. Some children within a group may be fairly slow at processing words and need simplified language, while other children in the same group may have quite sophisticated language. It is worth thinking about matching language levels to groups.

As part of the getting the language right, it is also important not to talk too quickly or continuously. Young children are often able to listen better when they hear short bursts of talk followed by a gap. This allows them to process the words and also to comment.

USING VISUAL ACCOMPANIMENTS

Children process words more easily when they are physically able to see the link between the word and its meaning. Children are more likely to listen and understand if we show pictures or get them involved in some way. This might also include gestures.

COPING WITH TALKING ALOUD IN LISTENING SITUATIONS

It is important not to reprimand children who need to talk in order to process what has been said. Ironically, when children are talking in response to something that has been said, it is a good sign because it means that the child has been listening to what has previously been said. It is important not to confuse listening with being quiet.

COPING WITH CHILDREN'S 'RANDOM COMMENTS'

Random comments are often thoughts that have appeared in response to something that the child has heard. There may be a direct connection, but there may not be an obvious one. If you are with the child, you can explore their comments, but in a group situation, you may decide not to do so at times.

BACKGROUND NOISE

It is important that we create opportunities for children to listen without the distraction of background noise. It is worth taking a reading of the noise level in your setting and then, if necessary, considering steps to reduce it.

ROLE MODELLING

Adults need to show how to listen by getting down to children's level, not interrupting and be interested in what children have to say.

Talking to parents

It is important to work with parents on children's listening skills. Firstly, we may need to check with parents about whether they feel there are any problems at home. It may be that children are fine at home because they are not in group situations and generally parents are using language that meets their children's needs. On the other hand, it may be that parents report that their child is not always responsive or does not appear to pay attention. If this is the case, it is always worth checking that a child does not have a hearing loss (see page 70). This is a common reason why parents report that their child has 'selective hearing'. It is also useful to share tips with parents about creating a good listening environment, by reducing background noise, as well as sharing with them what is typical development for the age of their child.

Losers (and winners)

While competition is part of life, some children find losing a game very difficult. They may sulk, throw a tantrum or if they win, they may be very arrogant towards the other children. Learning how to lose, but also how to win with some grace, is an important social skill. Some children can also develop a fear of losing and so may choose not to participate in games.

Learning to win and to lose is an important social skill

Why some children are bad losers or winners

SELF-REGULATION

Coping with strong emotions requires a high level of self-regulation. When children win or lose a game, it is likely that there will be an emotional response. For children under three years, low levels of self-regulation are the norm. This means that in a game situation, children may become very distressed if they cannot win. As we have seen, self-regulation is also linked to language levels, and so children who have language delay may also find some games difficult to cope with.

PERFECTIONISM

Some children have high expectations of themselves and so want to 'be the best'. In some cases, this can be driven by parental expectations, but there are children who seem driven from an early age to set themselves high goals. Children who have this trait may decide not to engage in an activity unless they are sure that they will be able to master it and so may not want to engage with games.

COMPETITIVE

Some children are very competitive. They may try and make many things into a competition. This is often the case where a child has older siblings at home that they strive to keep up with. Being competitive is not necessarily a bad trait as it can push children to achieve. It is important for children who are competitive to learn how to control their emotions when they win or lose.

LEARNED BEHAVIOUR

Some children may have developed habits about how to respond if they lose. It may be that at home or in the setting, a child who has lost learns that a tantrum or significant sulky behaviour results in plenty of adult attention or being then allowed to win the game.

BAD EXPERIENCE

Some children learn about how to lose or win from copying others. They may have experienced an older sibling who has won a game taunting them, and repeat this behaviour when they win. Some children may also be bad losers or reluctant to try a game because they have been teased when they are losing by other children or, surprisingly, by key adults in their lives.

How to respond

There are a few ways in which we can respond, but it is important to note that learning to lose and win and coping with these feelings will take time for children to master.

STEPPING IN QUICKLY

If a child who has won a game starts to be rude towards others, it is important to step in very quickly but calmly. You could say something such as 'I know that you are pleased that you have won, but remember to stay polite'. Simply stepping in quickly can prevent the child from becoming overexcited. In the same way, you should monitor the reaction of children who have lost the game. Note their colour, body language and facial expression. You can try saying something such as 'how are you feeling? Disappointed, perhaps?' as ideally, we need to help children recognise their feelings before helping them find ways of managing them. It is also asking children about what they might be able to do next to make themselves feel happier.

KEEPING CALM

If you were not able to step in quickly, the key way to respond is to quickly calm things down. This might include taking the child away from the situation so they can be distracted or, if they have sufficient language, to talk things through.

RESPONDING DURING THE GAME

It can be worth talking to children about other things during a game. This might include what they might do once the game is over. Focusing them on other things can be a useful distraction. If we know that a game is becoming tense, we can always create a pause. This is a good strategy for some children as it can help them to reduce their anxiety.

How to help children learn to win and lose with grace

In some ways, it is better to work on helping children learn how to win and lose well from an early age. There are several strategies that we might use for this.

ROLE MODELLING

It is important that we, as adults, show children how to win and lose gracefully. We can say things such as 'I don't like losing, but it is nice to see George winning. Congratulations, George'. We can also use role modelling to help children evaluate what has happened: 'This is a game where luck matters and I was not lucky' or 'I think that George was the better player this time'.

HELPING CHILDREN TO REFLECT ON THEIR PERFORMANCE

It can be worth helping children reflect on their performance when games involve tactics or physical skill. It might be that children can think about which areas of skill they need to practise, or to understand that another child is older and has already developed skills or tactics. Helping children to reflect on their performance can prevent children from giving up or coming to the conclusion that they are 'no good'.

PRAISING CHILDREN WHO WIN AND LOSE WITH GRACE

It is important to positively acknowledge with a comment those children who win and lose with some grace. Comments such as 'I know that it is not fun to lose, but well done for staying calm' or 'George, well done for saying "better luck next time" to Jake'. By praising children who win gracefully, other children are more likely to copy their actions.

AVOIDING LARGE GAINS AND LOSSES

Children are more likely to find losing difficult if the game they play is very intense or if there is a big prize on offer. As learning to win and lose with grace is partly about self-regulation, it is important to keep things very low key with young children who may not have good self-regulation skills.

USING PUPPETS

Puppets can be a great way of helping children to talk through the issues around winning and losing. This strategy works well with children who have some language. You can use the puppets to tell a story about someone who wins a game and boasts, or a story about a bad loser. If you decide on this strategy, it is important to talk about feelings and allow time for children to make comments. You can also use the puppets as a way of role modelling how to win or lose with grace.

Q

We have a fun sports day in the summer, but we find that some parents put a lot of pressure on their children to win. We are afraid that it undermines a lot of the messages that we are trying to give children. What should we do?

This is not unusual to find these days, and indeed some parents go into training in order to win the parents' race. One strategy might be to consider reformulating your sports day. Perhaps, it needs to be more low profile and combined with an afternoon of dance, reading, music or mark making. You may also need to let parents know about the aims of sports day and to include plenty of teamwork challenges. You may also like to have stickers for children who show great sporting manners, e.g. cheering on others, participating and showing generosity towards others. You could also have a quiet word with those parents who you know from past experience may overstep the mark.

A

USING GAMES

We can help young children learn to win and lose by devising some small, quick games that do not necessarily involve skill and where there is nothing in it for the winner. You could put a single wooden bead in your hand and clench it. Put out both of your hands and then ask the child to choose a hand. Sometimes the child will choose the hand but not at other times. When the child has not chosen the hand with the bead, say something such as 'Bad luck! Try again?'.

PLANNING AHEAD

If a child has good language, we can plan ahead with them about strategies that they may use to help them cope with losing. This works well with older children as it is a way of empowering them. A child might decide that holding a natural sponge and squeezing it hard when they feel upset might be the way forward.

Talking to parents

While it may not seem a serious issue for some parents, it is important to let parents know if children are struggling with learning to lose or win with grace. A good starting point is to ask whether parents always let their children win. This is commonplace in families with single children or where the child is the 'baby'. If this is the case, you could advise parents to occasionally put their child in situations where they do not win.

Some parents are also very competitive and have high expectations for their children. They may say that their child has to learn how to win. This is a sensitive area as parents may not appreciate the value of 'soft skills'. For some parents, it can be helpful to explain how 'soft skills' are valued by employers and also form part of many interview processes.

Lying

Once they begin to talk, most children will lie at some point. Most will lie to deny that they have done something that will get them into trouble, but others lie to draw attention to themselves, e.g. children may boast.

Interestingly, the topic of lying can open up a whole area of debate. Many adults routinely lie, although we may not recognise it as such. How many people have said that they are pleased with a gift when they are not, or have exaggerated an incident in order to entertain others? The reality is that few adults always tell the total truth, especially if this means upsetting someone. This means that the issue that children need eventually to learn is when and which lies are socially acceptable. This is a whole philosophical debate. Personally, I suspect that lying to save someone's feelings is probably acceptable, provided that the lies are not huge, while lying to gain advantage or to escape responsibility is not.

Why children may lie

There are many reasons why children may lie. It is important to think about these when children do lie.

GAINING ATTENTION

One of the reasons why some children lie is to gain adults' or other children's attention. They may realise that saying something of significant interest will provoke undivided attention.

MIMICKING OTHERS

Some children say that they have done something or that they own something because they have heard this from another child. They may have seen a positive reaction from their peers or the adult to what the other child has said and so realise that this is a way of getting the admiration of others.

TO AVOID A REPRIMAND

Some children will lie because they know that otherwise they are going to be in trouble. They may lie impulsively without thinking about how easy it will be for the adult to detect the lie or further consequences.

TO AVOID DOING SOMETHING

Some children learn to tell a lie to avoid having to do something. They may go to the toilet when it is time to tidy up or say that they are feeling poorly because they do not want to go outside. Children who say that they feel poorly in response to a situation are likely to be anxious.

How to respond

How you may respond to a child who is clearly lying will depend on the reason for the lie. Having said this, however irritated you feel, it is important to remain calm, as children may start to increase their lying in response to feeling fearful of being caught out.

DISTRACTION

When a child is clearly saying something to get your attention or admiration from other children, it is worth not disputing it as this may prompt the child to lie further. Instead, it is worth moving the conversation on and so taking the attention away from the child. You may also need to think about whether the child is in need of more positive attention and whether you need to find ways of making them feel special.

MOVING THINGS ON

If children deny doing something to avoid a reprimand, or come up with an alternative story, it is worth re-framing the conversation and moving things on. You could say something such as 'it doesn't matter now. Instead we need to think about how to put things right and stop this from happening again'. Later on, once the issue has been sorted, it might be appropriate to re-visit what happened and to let the child know that lying is not a good idea.

CLARIFYING

If you suspect that a child is lying to avoid doing something, it is worth saying something to clarify the situation, such as 'I think that you want to go to the toilet so that you don't have to tidy up. You can go to the toilet, but you will still need to help me tidy up'.

In the case of children who may be lying to avoid doing something that is a potential cause of anxiety, it is important to recognise this: 'I think that your tummy is hurting because you don't want to play outdoors'. It is also worth being vigilant when children lie to avoid going somewhere with other adults. While most adults are safe, sometimes a child's reluctance and anxiety can be an indicator of a safeguarding issue.

Talking to parents

Some parents become very anxious if their child lies. They may be concerned that this will lead to later problems. It is important therefore to reassure parents that it is fairly common in children and to share with them some of the strategies that we looked at earlier. For children who are lying to impress others, it may be that we need to work together to make children feel more confident so that they will not feel the need to make things up.

Preventing children from lying

As well as responding at the time to lying, it is also worth thinking about how you can prevent children from lying.

PREVENTING LYING FOR ADMIRATION

In terms of children who lie to gain others' admiration, you may wish to reflect on the practice within your setting. What happens when a child reports that they have done something extraordinary with their parents or there has been a significant life event? It may be that some children have learnt that others get a lot of interest from adults for saying something dramatic. While it is important to show interest in the life events of children, we must make sure that we show the same level of interest and excitement in the 'ordinary' lives of other children.

DON'T PUT CHILDREN IN A POSITION WHERE LYING IS AN OPTION

If you have seen a child do something or know that a child was involved in some way, it is worth making a statement to that effect, i.e. 'You threw the crayons on the floor. That was not helpful'. If, on the other hand, you ask the child a question, 'Did you throw the crayons on the floor?', it gives the child an option to deny it and so can help them learn to lie.

RESPONDING TO ACCIDENTS OR INCIDENTS CALMLY

Children are more likely to lie if they have done something unwanted or an accident has occurred because they fear adults' responses. If children learn that adults are quiet, calm and fair and that they listen to them, they are less likely to decide to lie. It is also important that with young children, reprimands or consequences are short-lived.

Mealtimes

Given that food and water are essential to life, it is surprising how many problems arise during meal and snack times. It is very easy for mealtimes to become a battleground instead of a happy, social occasion. Parents, in particular, can become very anxious and also frustrated when their children are not eating as they expect. This is because love and food are interlinked.

To help parents and children, it is worth doing some background reading about food and nutrition so that both the advice and the food you give is appropriate for the age and stage of the child. A good source of information is the Caroline Walker Trust who produce a range of resources that may help you and parents. (See **www.cwt.org.uk**.)

In this section, we look at four common challenges:

- **Food refusers**
- **Fussy eaters**
- **Slow eaters**
- **Table manners**

Food refusers

(see also p. 112 fussy eaters)

Food refusers, unlike fussy eaters, will not eat at all and will become very distressed if made to sit and eat. Fussy eaters, on the other hand, will eat providing that they are comfortable with the food that is available. When a child refuses to eat, adults can quickly become anxious and also frustrated, which in turn can compound the problem.

Why children may refuse food

There are many reasons why some children may refuse to eat while they are in a setting, although the basis of food refusal is anxiety. When some children are anxious, they lose their appetite and may actually find the process of eating and digesting difficult. Some children may also vomit afterwards. The trick is to work out with the parents what may be triggering the child's anxiety.

ATTACHMENT

Children who do not have a strong attachment to their key person will be more stressed and so be likely to refuse food. This is because some children can only eat when they are feeling relaxed. It is worth thinking about the quality of the key person–child relationship and also how much time a child is spending with their key person. In particular, think about how easily the child comes into your setting and how happy and relaxed they appear. Think also about how they seem when their parents pick them up. If children become angry, very clingy or upset, it may be that the child has not yet developed a strong attachment to their key person. If this is the case, you will need to think about strengthening the relationship or starting over with a new key person (see page 30).

BAD EXPERIENCE

Some children start off by not refusing food but then become food refusers as they have had a bad experience. It is worth thinking about what may have triggered food refusal. Here are a few suggestions of common experiences that may trigger food refusal.

Too much pressure
A child may have been told to eat quickly or too much food was put on the plate and the child became fearful.

Reprimand
The child may have been reprimanded during a meal or the 'spill over effect' occurred (see page 41) and another child was reprimanded. This experience may have caused the child to associate food with feeling uncomfortable.

Vomiting
The child may have eaten but then vomited shortly afterwards. This may have set up an association between feeling poorly and eating at the setting.

Noisy or overwhelming environment
Some children may refuse food because the environment in which it was served was intimidating in some way. This can occur in schools where many children may eat at once and the child may have felt overwhelmed.

CONSTIPATION

Sometimes when children are constipated, they may refuse to eat. This might be because the constipation has reached a critical point or that the child has realised that when eating, the digestive system starts to kick into action and they will be forced to go to the toilet. It is therefore always worth talking to parents about whether this is a possible cause, as they will need to get medical advice promptly.

NOT HUNGRY

If children are sessional, it may be that the child is simply not hungry because they have had a large amount of food just before arriving. It is not uncommon for some parents to still be giving food to their children on the way to the setting. This means that for a couple of hours, at least, the child will not necessarily be hungry.

ATTENTION SEEKING

Occasionally, food refusal originally caused by anxiety may develop into attention seeking if children know they will get a lot of attention from adults.

How to respond

As we have seen, there are several reasons why children may become anxious about eating, and so the starting point will be to piece together reasons why the child may be refusing food and to work on these.

This is a behaviour where it is important to work closely with parents and, if necessary, to quickly seek further professional support, especially if food refusal is also occurring at home and if the child is losing weight. It is also worth gaining professional support if a child who spends several hours in the setting is not drinking. Anxiety about food can quickly turn into a significant problem for the child and their family and so it is always worth encouraging the parents to get help promptly.

The key way to respond when a child refuses food is to stay calm and not make an issue about it. It is important that the child is not made to feel bad about not wanting food as this can increase their anxiety. Ironically, promising children something if they eat may not be such a good idea, as children's desire to get the sticker or promised resource may cause the child to become anxious. In addition, reducing the fuss and attention around the child may also reduce the likelihood of this becoming an attention-seeking behaviour later. As attachment issues and anxiety are usually the main cause, it is always worth providing plenty of positive attention away from the meal and snack times.

Changing the script

Once the source of a child's anxiety has been dealt with, we may then have to think about how to introduce a child to food in a new way. This is because, while the original anxiety may have been dealt with, a child may still associate meal and snack time with feeling stressed. The 'change the script' approach means creating a different experience for the child so that they can learn a new response towards food in your setting. It is worth talking to parents and also being creative. Here are a few suggestions that you might like to think about.

OUTDOORS

If food is served indoors, you could think about serving it outdoors as a picnic.

COOKING ACTIVITIES

Many children will eat as they cook. Think about some simple cooking activities where the child and one or two others can help you to prepare food.

ROLE PLAY

You could consider putting real food in the role play area, e.g. a slice of orange on a plate in the role play area or a tiny sandwich. You could also create a teddy bears' picnic with real food or put out superhero props including superhero plates with a little food on them.

PRIVATE DINING

Some children who are anxious may start out by eating in private. Consider creating a cosy space where there is a little food out and where adults keep their distance.

> **Talking to parents**
>
> It is important to talk to parents very early on when children are refusing food. As we have seen, food refusal is usually linked to anxiety and may have many causes. If parents are struggling with it at home or their child is a fussy eater at home, it is important that they seek professional help. It is also important to keep in close contact with parents so that they know whether their child has eaten and can ensure that the child's energy requirements are being met.

Cooking activities can encourage children to relax and eat

Fussy eaters

Fussy eaters are happy to eat, but only foods that they are familiar and comfortable with. Fussy eating is likely to occur at home as well as in the setting, and so it is important to work closely with parents. As with food refusal, it is important that professional support is sought quickly if the child is eating a very restrictive diet or is losing weight.

Why children may show this behaviour

GENETIC AND ENVIRONMENTAL FACTORS

While it is normal for children to have food preferences, some children can become very fussy eaters and very adverse to trying out new foods and textures. It is useful to understand that some children are born being very sensitive to texture, taste and smell. This means that they will be more prone to fussy eating. For other children, environmental factors such as when and how they were weaned can be the origin of fussy eating.

MEDICAL FACTORS

For some children, there are medical factors such as being tube fed, tongue tied or having gastro-intestinal problems which make fussy eating more likely. Some children may also associate food with vomiting or feeling poorly. If this is the case, it may be that advice will need to be sought from other professionals about how best to proceed.

AGE AND STAGE OF DEVELOPMENT

It is thought that the peak of fussy eating occurs at around two years. Foods that have been happily eaten before may start to be rejected, and children may refuse to try anything new.

ATTENTION SEEKING

Some children may use food refusal as a way of gaining adult attention. If this is suspected, it is important that, in addition to reducing the amount of fuss around meal and snack times, children are provided with plenty of positive attention at other times.

How to respond

The key to fussy eating is to remain calm and to avoid conflict at all costs. This is important as otherwise children begin to associate mealtimes with stress and so may even start to reject foods that they were comfortable with. If food is unwanted, the best strategy is to simply remove it and say something such as 'you don't want to eat that today'. This leaves the door open for the child to try it another day. Forcing a child to try something tends to backfire because the child will associate the food with being under pressure and develop a more hostile attitude towards it. Simply removing the food without any fuss also prevents children from learning to refuse food to gain attention from adults. It also prevents mealtimes from becoming a battleground.

Supporting fussy eaters

There are a few strategies that we can use to widen children's food choices, although no single strategy will be a quick fix. Patience as well as quiet persistence is required.

FAMILIARITY

Firstly, it would appear that familiarity with a new food makes a difference. In the case of fruit and vegetables, you could encourage children to handle them either as part of a cooking activity or even in role play. If you are able to take the children to the shops, you could encourage them to put them in the shopping basket along with a couple of other items and take them to the till. It is also important to keep putting out small quantities of the food at mealtimes even if it keeps being refused.

SMALL QUANTITIES

After being introduced to a new food, children need to repeatedly try it. Cut it up into tiny portions and let the child self-serve. Encourage the children to have a quick taste, even if they want to spit it out, but do not bribe them using other foods.

VARIETY

Children seem to be more likely to try out different foods if there is a colourful variety on offer. This might mean putting out a fruit platter or a dish with separate sections that have different vegetables on offer.

EMPOWERMENT

Children are more inclined to try out things if they are not feeling pressurised. Encouraging children to self-serve and also not focusing or saying anything about a particular food can help. You can also put out a range of different sauces, skewers or dishes so that children can choose how to eat it.

REGULAR MEALS AND SNACKS

It would appear that children are more likely to refuse food if they become over-hungry, so do plan out meal and snack times carefully.

KNOWING ABOUT QUANTITY

It can be helpful to look at nutritional guidelines from organisations such as the Caroline Walker Trust. Look out for their 'Eating well for 1-4 year olds: Practical guide' which shows typical portion sizes. Sometimes, children may not feel like trying new food because there is already too much on their plate.

FLEXIBLE APPROACH

It is useful to be flexible in your approach at meal and snack times. A child may eat up peas but only if they are in a separate bowl, or a child may eat a sandwich by eating the bread before the filling. A child who will not eat carrots, may like to try them raw.

BEING WITH OTHERS

It can be useful trying out new food in a group where you know that the rest of the children will have a go. This can help the child to feel more confident.

Q

We have one parent who is very anxious about her child's food intake. She checks through our menus and tells us what things her child won't eat. We find that usually, her child will try quite a few things, but apparently the child is very difficult at home.

When parents become anxious around mealtimes, this can make children with a propensity to be fussy eaters more anxious. It may be an idea to talk to the parent about what foods she would like her child to eat and see if you can try them out in the setting. This way the child will become familiar with them and less likely to refuse them at home. If the parent is very concerned about her child's diet, it may be useful to suggest that the parent contacts a health visitor.

A

Talking to parents

Parents can become very anxious about their child's eating habits, and mealtimes can quickly turn into a battleground. If this has started to be the case, it is worth encouraging parents to get professional help, especially if the child is starting to look ill or is losing or not gaining appropriate weight. It is also worth sharing some of the strategies that we have looked at, as well as signposting organisations such as the Caroline Walker Trust (**www.cwt.org.uk**).

Slow eaters

Some children seem to eat very slowly and are still ploughing through their meals long after the other children have gone. While anything up to 45 minutes is not atypical, once mealtimes reach an hour or more, there may be an issue. It will be important to find out whether slow eating occurs at home and whether it has always been a feature for the child.

Why some children may eat slowly

AGE AND STAGE OF DEVELOPMENT

The group of children who are likely to eat relatively slowly are likely to be 18 months–3 years. This is because the developmental skills involved in eating independently are still evolving. Children may also eat more slowly if the tables and chairs are too high for them as it makes it harder to use the utensils. Children may also struggle to eat if the utensils and cutlery provided for them are not appropriate for their age or stage.

TYPE OF FOOD SERVED

Some food is easier for children to manage than others. It is important to consider not just the quantity of food but also the consistency and combination of foods on the plate. Soft food that does not require chewing will often slip down easily but be aware that children need opportunities to practise chewing.

SOCIAL INTERACTION

Sometimes, children may be so engaged with others, that they may not take time to eat. As social interaction is something that is precious and in general something to be encouraged, unless mealtimes are very extended, action may not be needed.

DIFFICULTIES WITH CHEWING OR SWALLOWING

Some children may have physical difficulties in chewing or swallowing. If there are concerns shared also at home about the length of time that a child takes to eat, it will be worth seeking professional advice.

FUSSY EATERS

Some children who are very slow to eat may actually fall into the category of fussy eaters. They may be trying to delay eating foods that they are unsure about or dislike.

ATTENTION SEEKING

Some children learn that if they eat slowly, an adult will stay with them and they will gain plenty of attention.

LACK OF APPETITE OR TOO MUCH FOOD

The timings of meals and snacks are important. Children who are not sufficiently hungry may struggle to eat. Too much food on a plate can also put children off. It is important to look at the nutritional guidelines to check that the right portion size is being provided.

CONSTIPATION

Constipation can cause children to eat slowly, as either they already feel full or can start to feel that their digestive system is whirring into action, and they are afraid of passing a stool. If a child is constipated or showing the early signs of it, it is important that parents seek medical advice quickly.

ANXIETY

Sometimes children may be feeling anxious at mealtimes. This anxiety may make it hard for them to swallow, or they may lose their appetite.

TIRED OR OVER HUNGRY

Children who are tired or who are over hungry may not feel like eating. Tired children in particular may find the 'mechanics' of independent eating too much for them.

FINISHING EVERYTHING ON THE PLATE

Some children have learnt that they need to finish everything on their plate. This is because either they have received a lot of praise for doing this or this is the expectation in their home. Some children therefore continue to eat even though they are no longer hungry.

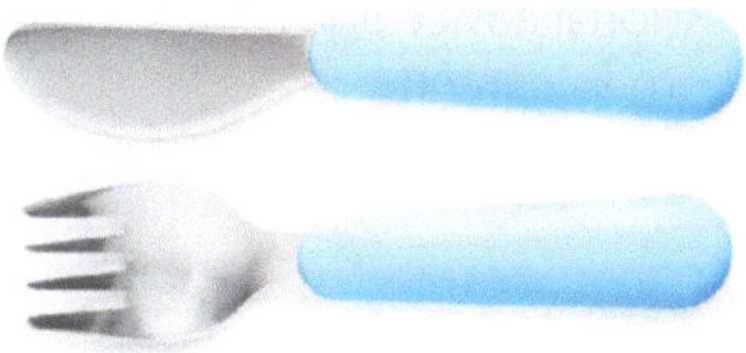

How to respond

There is no single way to respond as it will very much depend on the cause. Overall, it is important not to increase the anxiety of children or to lose sight that mealtimes should be relaxed and happy. Usually, there is no real problem unless the child is very underweight and eating so slowly that it is affecting their capacity to take in adequate amounts of food.

AGE AND STAGE OF DEVELOPMENT

It is worth making sure that expectations are appropriate, so that children are not struggling with the mechanics of putting food in their mouth. Typically, most children at three years will be using a spoon or a spoon and fork. While it is a good idea to encourage children to develop their skills in using cutlery, it is important to balance this with the need for them to actually eat. It can be worth starting a meal with just spoon and fork, and once children have started to eat well, to then swap to knife and fork for a little time.

As chewing is also difficult for younger children, it is important to cut meat and other items that require chewing into small pieces, and also encourage the child to combine it with other foodstuffs. It is easier, for example, to eat a small piece of meat alongside a small piece of potato. You may also need to consider getting the balance of chewy foods and easier foods right.

LISTENING TO CHILDREN

It is important to ask children who are eating very slowly whether or not they are still hungry. Some children are made to sit at home until everything is finished on the plate and so may think that they cannot stop until it is all finished. If children say that they are no longer hungry, encourage them to leave the table without making them feel that they have failed or that there is an issue. If there are concerns about the quantity of food that they have eaten, you can always ask them after twenty minutes whether they wish to return.

Children are more likely to try out new foods if they feel in control of portion sizes

SELF-SERVICE OR SMALL PORTIONS

It can be helpful for children to be given opportunities to self-serve or for adults to put small portions of different foods on the plate. This can prevent children from feeling under pressure. Dishes that have several compartments are also useful as children can feel that they are making progress.

AVOID FOCUSING ON EATING

It is important that adults do not make comments about the speed at which children are eating or how they are eating. This is important because any pressure on children can quickly create anxiety, and this in turn can cause further problems.

BEING FLEXIBLE

A flexible approach around mealtimes can help children immensely. It may be that a child would prefer to use a spoon to manage peas or would like a little help to cut up their food. While it is important that we strive for independent eating, there will be times when adults will need to feed a child who is tired or simply needs a helping hand.

Talking to parents

As with all food-related issues, it is essential to talk to parents about how their child eats at home and whether they have any concerns. It is helpful to find out whether the child has always eaten slowly or if this is a new trend. It can also be useful to know how parents manage mealtimes and if there are rules about leaving food. It is also helpful if parents know that food-related issues are a feature of life for most parents and that seeking professional advice is not a reflection on them as parents.

Table manners

Mealtimes are meant to be social occasions. Some practitioners and parents worry about children's table manners. This is a tricky area because table manners are not set in stone. They are conventions that vary between individual families, cultures and societies.

Why children may find it hard to show the table manners of the setting

DIFFERENT EXPECTATIONS

This is one area where expectations between individual families and the setting can be very different. The chart shows some of the key areas where expectations may be different, even between families of the same culture. It is helpful to talk to parents about their expectations when it comes to mealtimes.

Ways in which mealtime expectations can vary

Sitting at a table	Some families do eat at a table. Some eat food on their laps sitting on a sofa or chair. Other families may, for cultural reasons, sit on the floor.
Waiting for others	Not all families expect either to eat together or to wait for others to be ready before starting to eat.
Asking to leave the table	Some families insist that children have to ask to leave the table, while others have no particular rules.
Using cutlery	Some families, for cultural reasons, use their hands for eating. Others may use spoons or chopsticks. Some families eat primarily foods that do not require cutlery, such as burgers or sandwiches.
Eating independently (from two years)	Some families encourage their children to be independent from an early age by, for example, only helping them if necessary. Others may feed their children by, for example, spoon feeding them.
Eating quietly	Some families expect children to learn how to eat quietly, e.g. not slurping drinks and eating with their mouths closed. This is not the culture for other families.

Mealtimes

AGE AND STAGE OF DEVELOPMENT

As well as significant differences between individual families, the age and stage of children also makes a difference. We have seen earlier on page 115 that children's physical skills to handle cutlery develop slowly, and so this also makes a difference to the table manners that children can show. In addition, toddlers may not have the self-regulation skills to wait for a long time if food is in front of them.

IMITATING OTHERS

Mealtimes are social occasions, but this can mean that sometimes children can copy other children's behaviour and can become overexcited.

How to help children learn about table manners

It is important not to make a big deal about table manners as, for young children, there is a danger that anxiety about how to eat prevents them from enjoying the food. It is also important to find out from parents when children first arrive about how food is served at home and what expectations are in place. This is important because if the expectations are very different, children may take a time to adjust.

Talking to parents

This is one area where you may feel that parental involvement is not necessary as provided that in the setting there is a consistent approach, over time children will pick the customs and manners that are appropriate in your setting. If you feel that you need to talk to parents, a good starting point is to find out what their expectations are at home and the goals that they have for their children. In some cases, this discussion may prove helpful if your approach is quite similar overall. If parents' expectations are very different, you may need just to let them know what you are encouraging in the setting and agree that the child will gradually work out a 'dual system'.

Running indoors

Many practitioners find that children tend to run indoors rather than walk. In order to prevent collisions or accidents, this is a behaviour that might need to be curbed.

Why children run rather than walk

In some ways, running is part of childhood. It can be useful, though, to look at why young children find it so hard to walk rather than run indoors.

ENTHUSIASM

Many children will run because they are simply enthusiastic about what they are about to do next. It is easy to forget, but for many young children, things are simply exciting.

FEEL-GOOD FACTOR

Running is one of those 'feel-good' activities that is self-reinforcing. Running increases blood flow and heart rate and so arouses children. This is why young children often run ahead of adults when they are out and about.

Most children love to run as it gives them a good feeling

FEAR OF MISSING OUT

Some children want to be the first to get there or run across a room because they don't want to miss out on resources or an activity.

IMITATING OTHERS

Once three or four children start to run indoors, it is likely that other children will soon start to copy them. This creates a more frenetic atmosphere and can lead to children becoming overexcited.

Responding to children who run

We have to be careful not to overreact when children run. While it is important that they move carefully around, at the same time, running is part of childhood. It is often easiest just to block children's way and remind them to walk, then praise them for doing so. It is also then worth looking at ways to encourage safety indoors.

Helping children to move safely indoors

LAYOUT

One of the easiest ways of preventing children from running is to think carefully about the layout indoors. Some settings inadvertently create motorways and/or roundabouts for children by leaving long corridors of space or putting a piece of equipment in the centre, i.e. indoor slide. If you are frequently telling different children not to run, changing the layout is your first port of call. Start by watching children and how they move in the setting. How and why are they moving? Think about breaking up straight lines by putting a few obstacles in place. Think also about re-positioning some areas and resources, e.g. placing activities requiring water near a washbasin and aprons so that children do not need to crisscross spaces to get resources.

Running indoors

POSITIVE ACKNOWLEDGEMENT

Many settings will tell children not to run but will not say anything to encourage the walkers! This means that adults are often reacting rather than being proactive. While positive acknowledgement will not totally solve the problem, it can make a significant difference, as once some children start to walk, others are more likely to follow.

FOOTPRINTS AND LINES

Many settings find that if they put a line of tape down or some footprints, children tend to focus on these and thus slow down. This is worth trying out, but unless adults role model using the lines and footprints, there is a danger that after a while, children no longer pay attention to them.

SUFFICIENT PHYSICAL ACTIVITY

Many adults underestimate how much physical activity young children need. Running indoors can sometimes be a result of children not having had the level of physical activity needed. It is worth being aware of which children walk to your setting and how much movement outdoors they take part in.

DISTRACTION

There may be areas within your setting where it is hard to simply create some obstacles and barriers, e.g. corridors. There may also be times when you have noticed that children are more likely to run. While you could remind children to walk, it is also worth distracting children so that they have something else to do other than run. This might include singing a song together, counting the number of pictures/doors/books that are on view, or pretending to be certain animals.

Q

We have one or two children who find it very hard to walk around in the setting. We have a large number of volunteers who do not always remind children that they should walk. What should we do?

Consistency is part of the answer to this as you have correctly identified. You may want to have a star chart for the volunteers as a joke to help them remember to remind children to walk. In addition, you should check that the children are getting sufficient physical activity. You may also wish to reflect on your environment and consider how you might create a few obstacles.

A

Talking to parents

While you might like to share with parents that their child is physically active, it is important not to make a big deal out of this. As most children's home are quite small, running indoors is not likely to be an issue. It is, however, important to let parents know about the guidelines for physical activity for young children, as some parents may be surprised that their child should, throughout the course of a day, be spending three hours involved in moderate physical activity.

Sharing (not)

Sharing resources, space and toys is all part of being together with others. It may seem simple enough to ask children to share, but the reality is that sharing can be quite complex. This means that there are times when children will find it hard to share. Sharing is also linked to turn taking (see page 143).

Why children may find it hard to share

There are several reasons why children may be reluctant to share with others.

AGE AND STAGE OF DEVELOPMENT

The most common reason in young children is developmental. With some exceptions, most children will not be able to share until they are three years old. This is because sharing is a social skill. It requires that a child understand another's point of view and also that they can act empathetically. It also requires children to suppress their impulses. Not taking or keeping everything is therefore quite hard until children's language and cognition skills have sufficiently developed.

TIREDNESS

Even when children are over three years old, there are likely to be times when children will not share with others. This is more likely when children are tired and their ability to self-regulate and control their impulses is lowered. It is always worth remembering that being with others and continually sharing will be hard work for children. After the seventh or eighth hour, children may have had enough.

SHORTAGE OF RESOURCES

With older children, not sharing is often linked to a shortage of resources. It is worth thinking about areas or resources where squabbles often occur. It may be that there are not enough bananas in the fruit bowl for every child to have one or sets of wheels to make up a much-wanted car. In some cases, children may have a project in mind that requires a large quantity of red bricks, and so they 'hog' them to make sure that they will have enough to finish.

VALUED RESOURCES AND OWNERSHIP

Linked also to a shortage of resources is the idea that some things, including spaces, are highly prized. Children, once they have acquired the high-status item or space, may be reluctant to give it up or allow someone else to join them. This is especially true of items that children feel belong to them or that they have brought in from home. In some settings, older children who are established in the setting may find it hard to share with younger or new children. This is because they may think of the resources or spaces as being 'theirs'.

Most children are over three years old before they can cooperate and share resources

How to respond

How you should respond will depend on the situation. As sharing is a social skill, the ideal is for children to view sharing as a positive act rather than a deprivation. This means becoming very cross or irritated with a child is likely to backfire in the long term.

AGE AND STAGE OF DEVELOPMENT AND TIREDNESS

If the child is too tired or too young to be able to share, you need to provide a duplicate resource or space, or distract the other child or children. Charging in and insisting that the child must share is likely to cause an unnecessary tantrum and so should be avoided. If, however, you feel that the child might be able to share with a little adult support, you could join the child and see if the child will share with you first before ushering in the other child.

SHORTAGE OF RESOURCES

If sharing is mainly linked to shortage of resources, you will need to explain that there is not enough for everyone and so there is a need to share. Ideally, it is worth being proactive about this and doing so before there is a squabble. If you feel the child has sufficient language and understanding, you can talk about how other children may be feeling as they cannot join in. You can also give the child the option of staying and sharing or going to another activity where sharing is not an issue.

SHARING ITEMS FROM HOME

Where a child has brought in an item from home and does not want to share it with others, you may wish to give the child a choice of either sharing it with others or playing alone with it – preferably out of sight of others. You may also wish to explain to other children that some items are 'special' and sharing is not always possible. You could also ask children about items or toys that they have at home that are 'theirs'.

OWNERSHIP OF RESOURCES AND SPACE

Where a child or group of children have taken ownership of a space or resource, because they have not had to share it with others before, you will need to explain that, although it is difficult, there are times when resources have to be shared. With children who have good language, you can give them the problem and see if they can find a solution, e.g. 'You have had a lovely time playing with the dough by yourself. Now there are a few other children who also want to play with it. Have you any ideas as to how we can make this right for everyone?'.

NON-SHARING TIME

If you have children who are with you for long periods, consider creating a system when children can play without sharing towards the end of the session. You could have trays onto which children can put resources or toys and take them away to play with alone. This system works very well when children are becoming tired and need some space to be alone.

RELUCTANT SHARERS

Where children are developmentally able to share, but are reluctant, you may need to stay with them to help them to share. Some children are initially reluctant but with praise and encouragement will eventually share. It is always worth finding out first why they do not want to share. It may be that they do not like the other child or they have a 'project' in mind. If a child over three years routinely finds it hard to share with other children and often moves off to be alone, it may be worth assessing other aspects of the child's social development and talking these through with the child's parents.

Encouraging children to share

There are a few strategies that we can use which will help children learn to share, but do remember that very young children will not have much capacity to share at times.

ROLE MODEL

It is important to role model sharing. This can begin with very young children, e.g. passing a child a toy, marker or book.

ACKNOWLEDGING EARLY SHARING

To help children learn that sharing is a valued social skill, it is important that any attempt at sharing is acknowledged. Babies and toddlers will routinely pass objects to adults during play or as they are feeding. Adults should show delight when an item is shared and 'mock' sadness if the child takes back the item.

SHARING ALONGSIDE AN ADULT

With two-year-olds or with children who have had delayed social skills, it is important to do activities where children can share alongside an adult. Look out for open-ended resources such as dough, water or sand where there is an abundance of material that children can pass to each other. When children do share, it is important to be very positive so that they develop an understanding that sharing is good.

SUFFICIENT RESOURCES

Sharing is always easier when there are plenty of resources, especially duplicate ones. Checking that you have sufficient resources, especially ones that you know to be popular with children, can help children to share more easily.

ADVANCE WARNING

Children can sometimes be surprised to find that they are expected to share. It is always worth warning children ahead of time that, sooner or later, they may need to share a resource or area with other children.

STORYTELLING

If children have good language skills, you can use storytelling or puppets as a way of helping them to understand the importance of sharing. You can tell stories that look at what it is like to see someone who has a lot of things and who will not share. You could also tell a story of someone who would not share, but then no one wanted to be their friend.

Talking to parents

If children are finding it difficult to share in the setting and otherwise their development seems fairly typical, it may be worth talking to parents about how things are going at home. If the child does not need to share toys or resources at home, it can be worth parents finding ways to role model sharing and to encourage the child to share during games or mealtimes. It is important that parents realise the effect of praise and encouragement as, for some children, sharing does not come very naturally.

In some cases, where there is some upheaval or tension at home, children may become less inclined to share, as possessions can represent security. If parents feel that this is the case, it may be worth suggesting to parents that they focus on some simple routines (see page 43) to help children feel more secure. This might include bedtimes, mealtimes and also a time when the child is getting some positive attention.

Sibling rivalry may also be the cause of children finding it hard to share, particularly where relationships have become very competitive. It is worth talking with parents about strategies to support sibling relationships. This might mean praising and rewarding siblings for doing things together and being cooperative.

Shyness

Some children may appear to be shy as they limit their interactions with adults and even other children. Parents may report that their child refuses to say hello to relatives or attend other children's birthday parties.

Why children may show shyness

There are a number of reasons why children may show signs of shyness.

AGE AND STAGE OF DEVELOPMENT

For some children, being reserved or even scared of unfamiliar adults is linked to their age and stage of development. Typically, from 18 months through until three years, most children will show signs of uneasiness when they meet someone who is unfamiliar to them or someone they do not see very often. This is likely to be an instinctive response which is designed to protect young children from straying or being taken by predators. The 'stranger danger' usually means that children will stop what they are doing and head for the safety of their parent or other familiar adult. It can take a while for children to then start engaging with the 'new person'. It is important to understand that this is a developmental behaviour and it is not helpful to start labelling a child as 'shy' in this period.

PERSONALITY TRAIT

Some researchers believe that introversion or shyness is an inherited trait but that the environment that children are in can make it more or less pronounced. When children are put under pressure to be more sociable, this ironically is likely to make them 'shyer'. In young children, we have to be careful about labelling children as 'shy' or conversely 'extrovert' as this in itself can cause children to behave in ways that correspond to the adults' beliefs about them. It is also hard to separate out whether a child's stage of development is causing the 'shy' behaviour or whether or not it is part of the child's personality. Some children may also behave very differently according to who they are with. A child who may come across as 'shy' in a large group setting may show more extrovert behaviour in a playground or in the park.

Most children before the age of three years will be unsure about strangers

SEPARATION ANXIETY

If young children are not properly settled into a setting and have a strong attachment to a key person, they may show signs of shyness. They may keep away from adults in the setting or limit their interactions to the strictly necessary. It is important to consider whether this is the cause of the child's behaviour as if it is, the child may go on to have longer-term emotional difficulties if an attachment is not formed quickly (see page 28).

SOCIAL ANXIETY

Social anxiety is different to shyness. Social anxiety is normally recognised in older children and teenagers. Social anxiety is linked to feelings of being judged, fear of failing and thoughts about others' expectations. Children may not want to eat in public, may have tantrums which are not age or stage typical and be very anxious about doing anything where others will look at them. If you work with older children, you may need to consider whether a child who is showing extreme signs of shyness may actually have social anxiety and may need a referral.

How to respond

Regardless of the cause of why children are showing shyness, the best response is to not force the child to engage and not to make a big deal out of it. This is important because if a child hears that they are 'shy', it can start to affect their self-concept. Some children can start to believe that they have a problem. Forcing a child to say hello or engage with another child or adult when they are unsure can backfire. Children are more likely to be anxious as a result and so start to feel uncomfortable. They may also start to feel that they cannot meet adults' expectations.

APPROACH OF ADULT

How adults approach children can also make a difference to their response. Adults who are too enthusiastic to greet children can actually put them off. This means that it can be a good idea to warn other staff or adults who are about to meet a child who appears shy, not to initiate conversation but instead to glance at the child, smile and then not to make any further attempts at initiating conversation.

DO SOMETHING!

When adults are engaged in an activity such as planting seeds or using a puppet, some children's curiosity will overtake their reticence. This means that sometimes instead of focusing on the child, it can be better to focus on an activity. When the child approaches, it is then a good idea to glance, smile and then to carry on with the activity. This can then feel less threatening for a child.

BE POSITIVE

Shyness is often seen as a problem. The reality is that being shy is not a problem in itself, and it is a misconception to see shyness as being a fault. One only has to imagine the world to be full of extroverts and party animals to see that attraction of having some people whose tendency is to be quieter and reserved! It is also a misconception to believe that shyness is about lack of confidence. This is not necessarily the case and indeed it can be 'louder' children who need a lot of attention from others who are, in reality, lacking confidence.

Q

We have a child who is shy. She is nearly four years old and will be starting school soon. We are due to have several visitors to the setting in quite a short succession of time. Should we keep her away from them or do we encourage her to meet them?

Meeting new people will be a challenge for a child who is shy, but it is important that children learn to manage such situations. You can make it easier for everyone by telling this child and the other children that there will be visitors to the setting, and explain why they are coming. When the visitors come, you can give her the option of coming to say hello or waving to them. Whatever you do, it is important that everything is kept low-key and that she is not put under pressure.

A

Talking to parents

Parents who are confident and appear extrovert are often seen as the problem if their child comes across as being reserved or shy. The idea is that they are dominating their child. This is very unhelpful and not likely to be the cause. The reality is that some children's shy behaviours will be age or stage related or situation specific. In some cases, shyness might be part of a child's personality, but we will not know this until the child is older. A good starting point is to talk to parents about how the child responds when they are with them. It may be that their take on their child's 'shyness' is quite different from yours. If this is the case, it may be that you will need to look at the quality of the key person–child relationship and also whether the environment for the child is working.

Where parents feel that their child is shy, it is useful to explain that taking pressure off children is usually the way forward. It is also helpful to caution them against talking in front of the child about their shyness, as this can make the child feel that there is a problem.

Squealing or screaming

Some children learn to squeal or scream using a high pitch. The sound is ear splitting and uncomfortable for adults. This squeal or scream is not used for distress. Children may smile afterwards.

Why some children squeal or scream

AGE AND STAGE OF DEVELOPMENT

This behaviour is not unusual in children before they are talking well, and so it is usually found amongst toddlers. Typically, the squeal or scream starts when toddlers are experimenting with their voices. Making a loud noise when you are a small person can be deeply satisfying. In addition, the sound is also likely to attract the attention of adults. Once this happens a couple of times, toddlers are likely to use it increasingly to gain the attention of adults.

SQUEALING OR SCREAMING IN OLDER CHILDREN

Some children also scream or squeal in excitement. Interestingly, a squeal or scream seems to be quite infectious and so a group of children will quickly start to squeal or scream when they are happy and excited – especially during role play or when chasing each other. There also seems to be an issue around gender in squealing. Girls are more associated with squealing and it is often seen by children as a sign of being a girl.

Children like to gain the attention of adults; toddlers sometimes do this by squealing

How to respond to squealing

The response to this behaviour depends very much on the age of the child.

BABIES AND TODDLERS

In toddlers, the advice is to ignore the behaviour and not provide any eye contact or acknowledgement during the actual sound. Instead, wait for the children to stop squealing and then pay attention to the child. Distraction can also be tried but may not work, as being loud is actually part of the fun for the child. Squealing can be quickly habit forming, as the act of squealing is satisfying and children learn that adults pay attention to them. It can take a couple of weeks for this habit to die down, but in this time, it is important that all adults are consistent in ignoring and not commenting on the behaviour. As squealing is associated with low levels of language, it is also important to consider whether children's language is developing at a typical rate and, if not, whether further support is needed.

OLDER CHILDREN

With older children, squealing is not necessarily a problem unless you have neighbours that will object or it affects other children. If you decide to intervene, it is important that you have a good reason, as children are just having fun. Reasons for curbing the squeal may include that other children are having a nap or a new child has started and may be upset by the noise.

Talking to parents

While squealing in older children is not normally a problem as such, it is important that squealing in babies and toddlers is discussed with parents. Squealing can be problematic for parents because they may be dealing with it when they are in public spaces. It is worth encouraging parents to be consistent at ignoring the actual sound but also to be proactive in providing positive attention.

Sulkiness or stroppiness

Some children protest by being sulky or stroppy. They may take themselves away from a situation or refuse to talk or engage with adults or other children. For some children, sulkiness and stroppiness can last quite a while.

Why children may sulk or be stroppy

Sulkiness or stroppiness is a form of protest. It is something that is usually seen in children who are over three years old.

TO SELF-REGULATE

Some children may withdraw from others as this helps them to self-regulate and come to terms with the situation. Where children feel that they have not been listened to or there is an injustice, it is likely that they will withdraw and sulk. It is therefore important that we are good at giving children chances to express their viewpoints.

ATTENTION SEEKING

Some children learn to sulk or be stroppy in order to gain the attention of adults or other children. When this occurs, there are often give-away signs. Children may half-smile at times or may look at what is happening with interest but then turn back and scowl.

TO CHANGE OUTCOME

Some children learn that being sulky or stroppy is a way of changing an outcome that they were not happy with, e.g. not getting a biscuit. Children will develop this as a strategy if they have had success at changing the outcome in the past (page 82).

TIREDNESS

As with many aspects of behaviour, tiredness will affect children's ability to moderate their reactions.

IMITATING OTHERS

Some children show sulky or stroppy behaviour because they have seen other children or even adults do it. They may have seen at first-hand how showing this behaviour can change outcomes.

How to respond to sulking behaviour

Being disappointed and not being able to do or have something is hard for children. Learning to spring back from disappointment and move on is a skill. There are many different ways in which we might need to respond to children depending on the context of why they are sulking or being stroppy.

ASKING CHILDREN ABOUT THEIR FEELINGS

It may be appropriate, where a child sulks who does not normally do so, to ask about their feelings. You may begin by making a comment which can act as an invitation for the child to respond if they wish, e.g. 'Things are not right for you, are they?' or 'It is hard when you cannot have something that you really want'. It may take a time for a child to choose to respond, but especially if there has been a perceived injustice, it is important that they are heard. It may be that they have not understood the context in which the decision was taken.

IGNORE AND DISTRACT

Where children are sulking or being stroppy to gain attention, or using it as a strategy to change the outcome, it is important that this behaviour is ignored while at the same time a distraction is provided. For some children who have protested very loudly and then sulk, it can be hard for them to 'save face'. Thinking of ways to help the child feel accepted and valued again will be important. You might say to a child afterwards, 'we have saved a place for you'.

RESPONDING TO OTHER CHILDREN'S CONCERN

Other children may also notice that a child has withdrawn and is in protest. It is important to reassure these children without demonising the behaviour. Comments such as 'Daniel was disappointed that he could not go first, but when he is ready, he will be fine' will help.

Preventing sulking and stroppiness

There are a few strategies that can be used to help prevent the need for children to feel disappointed and to sulk.

PREPARATION

Some children can be helped if they are prepared for what is about to happen. Parents may tell children that although last time they went to the cinema, they had an ice cream, this is the not the case this time.

LISTENING TO CHILDREN

When children first look bitterly disappointed and before they have gone into sulk or strop mode, it is worth listening to children and hearing what they say. In some cases, this might prevent an injustice. At other times, it may be that we need to acknowledge the child's feelings, e.g. 'I know that you wanted to be first on the bike, but it was Simon's turn. I understand that it is hard to have to wait when it is your idea'.

PROMOTING 'THINKING TIME'

While it is important that children do not learn that if they sulk, they can change outcomes or gain adult attention, we do need to teach children that reflection and taking time to process emotions is a positive strategy. We could call this 'thinking time'. We may use puppets or a story to illustrate how a character faced with a disappointment told his friends that he needed 'thinking time'. If we use a term such as this, we can then start to label it when we see it. So, if a child goes on in a huff, we might tell the other children that the child is engaging in 'thinking time'. Over time, some children may come to articulate that this is what they are doing.

Q

We have one child who is four years old. She is happy in the setting and has a few friends. She used to sulk a little in the setting, especially if the other children would not do as she wanted, but now she has moved on. At home, it is a different story. Why might this be?

This child has probably learnt from the reactions of the other children that sulking does not change the outcome. At home, she is probably still able to influence her parents and so the habit has continued. It may be worth letting parents how well she has come on in the setting and seeing if they wish to try some strategies at home. Consistency and patience will be the key, as it sounds as if this has become quite a habit.

A

Talking to parents

While most children at some time or another will take themselves off and sulk, where this has become a frequent habit and is being used either to gain attention or change outcomes, it is worth talking to parents. It is helpful to know whether these issues are occurring at home and how parents deal with it. In some cases, parents may say that they usually give in or other parents may say that they get cross with the child. It can be helpful to agree with parents an approach that can be used at home and in the setting. It is also worth keeping a log of how often and when the child goes into a sulk, firstly to see if there are any patterns and then to see if the behaviour becomes less frequent.

Swearing

Swearing is the use of words, usually sexual ones, that are offensive to others. Swearing is not an uncommon behaviour amongst young children in this day and age. This is mainly because society today is more tolerant of swearing and children are likely to be exposed to swearing at an early age. They may be with adults who routinely swear or they may hear it in the media or in public places.

Why children may swear

Children learn swear words by hearing others use them. It is interesting how easily young children can pick up swear words. This is sometimes because swear words are used in stressful situations and also because the words themselves sound strong. This combination means that children will be alerted to the swear words and so are more likely to learn them.

In addition, some children may be exposed to frequent swearing that is routinely used in the construction of sentences by adults or teenagers that they spend a lot of time with. This type of swearing is particularly difficult to tackle as it can become part of how children learn to talk.

How to respond

How to respond when you hear a child swearing will depend very much on the age of the child and also the context.

VERY YOUNG CHILDREN (0–2 YEARS)

With very young children, the key strategy is not to react in any way, even if it seems amusing. This is because, typically, a child will simply be unconsciously repeating something that they have heard. If there is any reaction, they are more likely to keep saying the word to get further reactions. You should also use distraction as a technique (see page 60).

ONE-OFF SWEARING (3–5 YEARS)

Some children may try out a swear word that they have heard just to see what happens. They may do this as attention seeking (see page 82) or to impress their friends. When 'one-off' swearing takes place, it is worth intervening, but doing so in a very gentle but firm way. Take the child to one side and tell them that they have used a word that is 'not nice'. Say that you are not cross with them, but tell them firmly that it is not to be used again.

COPYCAT SWEARING IN ROLE PLAY (3–5 YEARS)

Some children will swear while they are in 'role'. This may be directly linked to something that they have seen on a screen or a scene that has happened in real life. If other children are around, you should intervene promptly to avoid other children picking up this language; or you might want to just stand back and watch the scene to learn further about what the child has seen in case there is a safeguarding issue (page 82). Depending on the level of language and the role play scene that is taking place, you may want to ask the child about where they have heard these words. You will also need to tell the child that they have used words that are 'not nice' and be clear that they should not use them again.

FREQUENT SWEARING BEYOND THREE AND A HALF YEARS

As children's language moves towards fluent, you may find that a few children start to swear frequently, and it becomes part of their language style. If this is the case, you will need to take a long-term approach to changing this behaviour. The aim is to change the language style while maintaining the child's willingness to communicate. It will require much patience and, however distasteful it may seem to hear a child using bad language, it will be important for everyone to recognise this is copied behaviour and is unlikely to be deliberate.

You will need to decide how aware the child is that sentences and phrases contain swear words. If the child is not aware and you feel that the swearing is now established as a way of speaking, the best strategy is to keep recasting or repeating back what the child has said without the swear words. The idea is that by repeatedly hearing language without swear words, children may learn to drop these words while in the setting. Where a swear word is being used as a way of expressing frustration rather than in the make-up of a sentence, you should intervene and say that the word is not appropriate. You can also model language to use when frustrated to replace the swear word.

Other issues

There are some practical issues that are likely to arise if a child is swearing in a setting.

Firstly, other children are likely to come and tell you what another child has said. You should thank the children for their concern, but avoid making too much of it.

You may also find that some parents complain that their child has come home and used swear words. They may also pinpoint which child they feel is the source and ask you to intervene. As you have a duty of confidentiality, you will not be able to talk about other children, but you can give parents strategies for dealing with 'one-off' swearing and also explain how you are tackling the problem in the setting.

Preventing swearing

It is hard to prevent swearing from occurring as children are often copying behaviour from outside of the setting. While you would hope that all staff and volunteers are mindful of their language when they are with children, if you have a code of conduct, this should be incorporated into it.

Talking to parents

Swearing is a behaviour that requires sensitivity when feeding back to parents. If swearing is a 'one-off', it is important not to make a drama out of it. Just explain to parents what has happened and that this is not unusual, but share with them strategies that they can use at home.

Talking to parents about a child who is swearing frequently can be harder. A good starting point is to recognise that some parents may not share your point of view as to what is and isn't a swear word. It is also worth remembering that we cannot automatically assume that the child has copied the parents' language. It may be that the child spends time with older siblings, family members or friends who swear frequently. They may also be watching films or other media that is not age appropriate and includes swearing. Asking or implying to parents that they are responsible for their child's swearing is unlikely to be that useful. It can cause parents to become defensive and uncooperative.

It is therefore often better to couch the discussion in terms of everyone having different feelings about swearing while clearly explaining what your setting's policy is in relation to swearing and why. With some parents, you may also have to be clear about which words your setting considers to be unacceptable. It is also worth explaining to parents what the implications of continued swearing will be on how easily their child is accepted by others. Many parents do not realise that their child's friendships might be at stake or that, as they move into school, their child may be punished for inappropriate language.

Tantrums

Tantrums occur when children's ability to self-regulate and control their emotions has failed in some way. This results in children becoming very angry, distressed and out of control. Tantrums usually last a few minutes and, once under way, can be hard to curtail. Typically, you would expect to see tantrums from anywhere from 15 months through until three and a half years, although the majority of tantrums will be seen between two and three years.

Why children may have tantrums

Most tantrums are related to children becoming frustrated by a situation. It may be that a child has seen an object or toy and cannot have it immediately or that they want to do something and the adult or another child is preventing them. The majority of tantrums are developmental in nature. They are particularly linked to children under three years because, typically, children have less expressive language at this age and so cannot use language to negotiate or talk through their frustration. The strong emotions inside the child build up and boil over in an uncontrollable way. Where older children have not developed strong expressive language, it is likely that tantrums will persist and so it is not uncommon to find four or five-year-olds with lower levels of language still having tantrums (see Language, page 50). While tantrums can happen at any time of the day, children are more prone to tantrums when they are tired or hungry. One of the key features of a tantrum linked to development is its intensity and the way that an adult cannot reason, bribe or reassure a child during it.

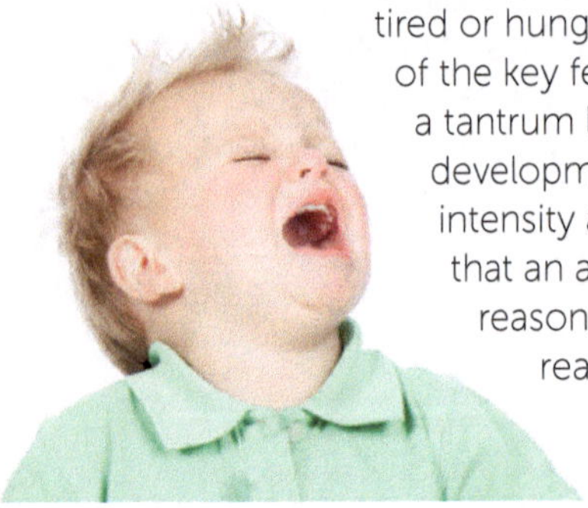

TANTRUMS WHEN CHILDREN HAVE GOOD LEVELS OF LANGUAGE

While most tantrums are part of a developmental stage, some children can get into the habit of having tantrums as a way of attention seeking, or as a way of asserting themselves over adults. In other cases, tantrums may be the sign of a child who is emotionally insecure. Working out what type of tantrum a child is having and the reasons for it is key to responding effectively.

ATTENTION SEEKING

Although in the majority of cases, language level is linked to a child having a tantrum, some children can learn to use tantrums as a way of getting attention from adults. Tell-tale signs that a tantrum is attention seeking include children checking that they have an audience, moving themselves from one place to another if the adult moves, and overall, a less intense tantrum. As with all attention-seeking behaviours, the way to reduce this behaviour is to give children far more attention at other times.

ASSERTING THEMSELVES

Children who have good levels of language but still have tantrums may have learnt that the threat of a tantrum or having a tantrum can change an outcome in their favour. Parents who are afraid of their child having a tantrum may, at the very first signs of a threatened tantrum, change a decision that they have made, and so the child develops this as learned behaviour. As with attention seeking, the chances are that the tantrum is less intense and violent than a tantrum linked to development. It is always worth talking to parents when this type of tantrum occurs and agreeing a consistent strategy together. This will usually involve agreeing not to give into the demands of the child, while ensuring that children in other aspects of their lives are being empowered (see also page 81).

EMOTIONAL INSECURITY

Children who are insecure because of a change in family circumstance or who do not have a strong bond with their key person may show tantrums. These tantrums are an expression of anxiety or anger and it is important that we recognise them as such. It is unlikely that these tantrums will be the only sign that a child is anxious or angry. One of the signs that a tantrum is linked to anxiety or anger is that the tantrum may occur for little or no reason and so be quite unexpected. It may also be out of character for the child. When children are showing this type of tantrum, it is important to find out as much information as possible from parents and also other settings that the child may attend. Reducing these tantrums may require that the child has more attention from their key person, strong routines as well are more opportunities to be empowered (see page 81). Some children may also need a referral to other professionals to unpick the deeper issues that are causing the child to feel so anxious or angry. Finally, while these types of tantrums may have a straightforward explanation, you should always be alert as to whether or not they are a symptom of a safeguarding issue.

How to respond

The golden rule during a tantrum is to stay totally calm. A child who is struggling to control their emotions needs to feel emotionally safe, and if adults raise their voices or become agitated in any way, it is likely to make the situation worse.

Strategies for responding during a tantrum will vary slightly according to the reason why a child might be having one. It is a good idea, though, for other children to be kept away and also for only one adult to be involved. It is also important that, during the tantrum, the adult stays near the child so as to be a reassuring presence.

Once most tantrums are under way, it is unlikely that touching or talking to the child will make much difference. Indeed, with some children, it may even prolong the length and intensity of the tantrum. After a tantrum is over and the child is calmer, with the exception of older children and where tantrums are linked to emotional insecurity, it is not usually helpful to make reference to it. Allow the child to recover and then pick up where things left off.

It is, however, worth reflecting on why the tantrum occurred and what it might signify. It may be that the child had become overtired or a situation was not handled well. Working out what the triggers are for individual children may help us to prevent further tantrums.

Q

We have a parent whose child regularly has tantrums. The parents want us to talk and cuddle the child during the tantrum. Is this a good idea?

There is a school of thought that suggests that holding a child during a tantrum can be helpful. In terms of your setting, I would be very careful about this as a strategy, as the chances are that the child will try and tear themselves away. If you were continuing to hold them, you would be in effect restraining them, and this should only be done when a child is likely to harm themselves or others. I would be more inclined to focus on the cause of the tantrums and to see whether they can be prevented from occurring.

A

Tantrums

Preventing tantrums

Some tantrums, especially ones linked to development, can be avoided or reduced if adults are proactive.

SLEEP AND HUNGER

Think about moving forward nap time or snack time to avoid children becoming overtired or hungry.

ROUTINES

Consider whether the demands made on children at different times in the session or day are appropriate. It may be that a child can share in the morning, but after nine hours, no longer has this capacity.

VISUAL TIMETABLES

Some tantrums are caused because children feel rushed or anxious. The use of visual prompts and also visual timetables can be very helpful with all ages.

FLEXIBILITY

Tantrums linked to development can sometimes be avoided if adults are flexible in their approach. The fewer 'no's that a two-year-old hears, the better.

REMOVING UNAVAILABLE ITEMS

Very young children find it hard to regulate their impulses. Seeing desirable items and then not being able to have them is very difficult for young children. While older children and those with good levels of language can be given an explanation, such as 'it is for later' or 'it belongs to someone else', this does not work very well for children under three years. Instead, it is worth trying to remove items that children will not be able to have.

Toys that are not suitable for these children were removed before they arrived

Talking to parents

Tantrums are one area where it is important to share information with the aim of understanding why tantrums are taking place. It is highly likely that this will be a behaviour that crosses over with the home and setting. As majority of tantrums are developmental, it is worth talking about the role of sleep, as well as language, in tantrums.

Whatever the cause of the tantrum, it is also useful if there is an agreed strategy in how to respond to tantrums that is consistent. As tantrums usually fade away rather than disappear abruptly, it can also be helpful to track the number taking place in order to recognise whether or not progress is being made.

Tidying up

Tidying up is an important social as well as practical skill. Tidying up allows others to enjoy the environment and resources. It also can play a part in children learning to self-regulation skills. Some settings find that some children are happy to play with materials, but do not tidy up afterwards. There may be a specific tidy up time or children may be expected to tidy materials once they have finished playing with them.

Why children may not tidy up

There are several reasons why children may not tidy up, although most of these are linked to the expectations of adults and also the environment that children are in.

AGE AND STAGE OF DEVELOPMENT

For most children (and even some adults), tidying up is not something that will occur naturally. Moving on to the next thing is likely to be children's default position. Tidying up is about self-regulation as it requires children to control their impulse to move on and do something more pleasurable. It will take many years before tidying up becomes automatic, and this will only occur if adults consistently encourage it.

OVERWHELMED

In some situations, children may not tidy up because they feel quickly overwhelmed by the quantity of toys and resources to be picked up.

EXPECTATIONS

Some children may not have realised that tidying is an expectation of the setting, especially if they are not required to do so at home. They may not have clear instructions or reminders about when they should tidy up.

A tidy environment can help children to concentrate

RESPONSIBILITY AND RECOGNITION

Where there is a 'group' tidy up time, some children are not given specific instructions as to what and where they should tidy. They may realise that no one notices if they do or don't tidy up well.

INCONSISTENT APPROACH

In some settings, there is an inconsistent approach towards tidying. Some days, it may have a high focus, but on others, children are not reminded to tidy away. There can also be very different approaches between staff.

How to respond if children do not tidy up

If children are not tidying up, you will need to think carefully about your environment, expectations and routine. In the short term, there are a few immediate strategies that you can try.

With very young children, the best way to encourage tidying up is to distract the child and begin to tidy up yourself. If you are occupied in tidying up and also turn it into an interesting game, many children will come and help for a little while. When this happens, it is important to be positive and encouraging.

Tidying up

With older children, you can try out the distraction technique first and if this does not work or if there are one or two children who are not joining in, you should give them specific but easily achievable targets for what they should tidy away, e.g. 'Sal, you need to put two cars in the box'. It is worth aiming for a firm voice, but avoid confrontation by smiling. You may also provide an incentive, e.g. 'once we have tidied up, we can see about getting the puppets out'. It is also important to provide positive feedback as the child is about to tidy or put something away 'great work, there!' or 'that's brilliant!'.

If children refuse to tidy up, it is worth ignoring the behaviour so that it does not become attention seeking. Sometimes, children when they see that others are being positively acknowledged will start to join in quietly.

How to encourage children to tidy up

ROUTINES

It is worth making sure that some everyday routines contain some tidying away. This might mean that children take their plates or cups to the side after they have finished or push in their chairs. Building tidying into everyday routines and calling it such can gradually create a culture in a setting of tidying.

CONSISTENCY AND ROLE MODELLING

It is important that adults consistently expect children to tidy away during the everyday routines to start with. They should also role model tidying at other moments, making sure that children's attention has been drawn to it.

CREATING AN EASY ENVIRONMENT FOR TIDYING

If we expect children to tidy away at specific areas such as role play, dough or the water tray, we have to make it easy for them. There are several ways that we can do this:

Container size
It is worth putting resources such as bricks, cars and farm animals into small containers so that children are not tipping out more resources than they can actually play with. It is also worth observing what specific items seem to attract children's attention and make these easy for children to find, e.g. which farm animals do children hunt for, or which of the boats do children actually play with in the water tray?

Less is more
Think carefully about how many resources of the same kind are needed in a play area, e.g. scissors, or cups and spoons in the role play area. Think about how many children are likely to be using the resources at the same time and adjust the quantity accordingly.

Labelling
Labels showing where things go and maybe even a number can be helpful. A pot with a photo of scissors and a number '5' can help older children to know that there should be five scissors in the pot.

Designated areas
It can be easier to tidy up if there are designated areas where resources 'live'. This works well for large objects such as pushchairs, trikes and balls.

Rotation of resources

There is a case for the rotation of resources so that not all is out at once. This can help resources to feel 'fresh' but also makes it easier to manage. If you decide to rotate resources, do create some photo books so that if children cannot see what they want to play with, they have a way of asking to get something out.

Sufficient storage

Some environments can feel untidy even before children arrive. This is often because there is not sufficient storage available. Focusing on storage and ease of use for children is therefore important.

REMINDING CHILDREN

While children are playing, it is worth reminding them what will need to be tidied away once they have finished. If there is a significant amount which might be overwhelming, you could suggest to children that they come and find you so that you can give them a hand.

GAMES AND MUSIC

There may be times when spaces need to be cleared to allow for mealtimes or for a change in activity. It can be useful to make this larger scale tidying up into a fun activity. You could put on music or play games involving the number of items to be tidied away.

EXPLAINING THE VALUE OF TIDYING UP

It is important that, over time, children come to understand the purpose of tidying up. Tidying up should not be associated with just doing what adults tell you to. You could tell a story about what happens when toys are left out or where pieces go missing.

PRAISE AND POSITIVE ACKNOWLEDGEMENT

Adults need to help children feel successful, and so praising children when they tidy up and acknowledging its importance is key. Some children may also need more tangible acknowledgement and so you may consider the use of stickers to get children motivated. If you decide on this type of 'concrete' reinforcement, you will need to think about how you will help children to maintain their enthusiasm.

Q

We currently have tidy up times at different points in our session. There are always a few children who manage to go to the toilet at these times or who wander around.

I personally prefer the approach of 'tidying as you go' with adults supporting children during the session. This does mean that the environment needs to be set up in a way that allows it to happen easily, e.g. considering the quantity of resources and how they are stored. If you take the whole-group approach to tidying up, it is worth allocating adults and teams of children to work together. This could be along the lines of key person groups. Each adult and 'their team' would be responsible for a particular area. This approach has the advantage that children cannot slip through the net and that they can get the support they need to tidy up. In some settings where this has been introduced, children have then sung rhymes or played a game in their small group.

A

Talking to parents

Children are more likely to find tidying up easier where there is a consistent approach. Ironically, sometimes, children at home can be tidier than in the setting! It is therefore worth agreeing some expectations with parents.

Toileting

Difficulties with toileting are often common in group care settings. While this is not a 'social skill' as such, it can lead to a child feeling anxious as well as create frustration in adults.

It is not uncommon for young children to have occasional 'accidents'. Where children are frequently having accidents, it is important to think about possible causes.

Why children may wet themselves

IMMATURE BLADDER

The developmental range of when children leave nappies is quite large. Anything between 18 months and three years would be normal. Typically, children should be able to retain urine for around two hours, and this is a good sign that a child is ready for toilet training. If children are having several accidents over the course of a couple of hours, it may be that their bladder is not sufficiently mature, and so they may be best going back into nappies until they can retain urine for longer periods.

NOT AWARE OF URGENCY OF A FULL BLADDER

Some children may become so engrossed in an activity that they may not realise the need to go to the toilet urgently. Some children may try to postpone a visit to the toilet if they are afraid that they will miss a turn or another child might take their place or toy.

URINARY INFECTION

One cause of more frequent urination is an infection of the urinary tract. This is more common in girls, especially if they are incorrectly wiping themselves after a bowel movement. In some cases, children may complain of pain on urination or they may develop a temperature but not always. If a child has previously been reliable, it is worth encouraging parents to check this out with their local GP.

ANXIETY

Some children become scared about going to the toilet away from home. They may be fearful in the new environment. Some children also find it hard to pass urine when they can hear other children or adults nearby.

ENVIRONMENT AND ADULT BEHAVIOUR

Some toilets are more inviting than others. It is always worth considering whether your toilets are 'child friendly'. It is also important to think about how adults remind children to visit the toilet or support them with dressing.

ASKING TO GO TO THE TOILET

While the ideal is always that children can freely access the toilets, this is not always possible in all settings. As children become more self-aware, some dislike and feel embarrassed asking if they can go to the toilet, especially if the adult seems to find it a nuisance to take them.

CONSTIPATION

Some children who become constipated resist going to the toilet because they know that this may result in the opening of the bowels, which will be painful. The fear of pain means that they may hold off for as long as possible.

How to respond to children

It is important to respond to accidents in a friendly calm manner. Once children start to feel 'shame', it can affect their confidence and they may develop an anxiety about going to the toilet. The first step is to keep other children away and get the child clean and dry. Allowing the child to be as involved as possible in washing and changing is important. It is also useful if there is a choice of underwear and clothes to help empower the child.

It can also be helpful to explain to children what has happened in a matter-of-fact way, e.g. 'I think that your wee-wee came out before you were ready'.

Once the child has been cleaned up, it is important to carry on the session and not refer to it again. Having said this, some children may feel quite shaken, and if this is the case, it is worth encouraging them to do something alongside you where you can give them some positive attention.

How to prevent accidents

There is no single way to prevent accidents, but there are several strategies that can be helpful.

TOILET TRAINING

It is useful if parents and all practitioners in your setting understand the importance of bladder maturity before taking children out of nappies. Everyone also needs to understand two children of the same age may have up to a year's difference as to when bladder maturity will be achieved.

ENVIRONMENT

It is useful to look at your toilets and think about how to help children feel positive about this space. In group settings where there may be several toilets, you could use different-coloured toilet seats or decorate the doors with different superheroes or images that will appeal to children. This can help to empower children as they can then choose which cubicle to go in.

REMINDERS

It is helpful for children who have had an accident to make sure that they get a discreet reminder about going to the toilet after a couple of hours when their bladder is likely to be full. Avoid continually reminding children to go though, as this can make them resentful.

ROUTINE

Some children benefit from routines such as going mid-morning after they have been in the setting for a while or before going outdoors to play.

STAR CHARTS

Star charts can be used as a way of motivating children who are delaying going because they are distracted by an activity (see page 88). They are not so useful for children who are only just toilet trained or during the toilet-training process.

Talking to parents

Let parents know that their child has had an accident and arrange to hand over the clothes discreetly and preferably out of earshot of the child. Some parents can feel very embarrassed or even angry that their child has had an accident. It is worth reassuring them that this is a fairly common experience.

It is important, if a child regularly has accidents, to talk about how things are going at home. It may be that there are no issues at home, in which case, you can use the strategies that we have already considered. If, on the other hand, the parent says that they have to constantly remind the child to go to the toilet or that the child has only recently started to have accidents, it may be worth considering whether there are other issues such as urinary infection, constipation or whether the bladder is sufficiently mature.

Q

We have a child who is now out of nappies but refuses to poo in the potty or the toilet. It is a problem at home as well. What should we do?

This is not unusual. Some children gain control of their bladder but become fearful about passing a stool. Unlike urine that cannot be stopped, children can actually choose to defer passing a stool. This can result in constipation which can be very difficult to deal with as well as painful for the child. Start off by checking with the parents that the child is not already constipated. If so, they should visit their GP. To avoid this from occurring, it is important to take a flexible approach when it comes to passing a stool. To start with, if a child wants a nappy, they should have it. Once the child has regained confidence, you could try putting the nappy on quite loosely so that the child can feel a stool falling. You could then move to lining the potty with the nappy so that the child has some of the feeling of the nappy. Some practitioners also find that cutting a large hole in the back of the nappy works well. These strategies may seem odd, but if they stop children from becoming constipated, they are worth it. The problem usually resolves itself as the child overcomes their fear.

A

Turn taking

Turn taking is a social skill. It is one of the most frequently used skills when with others and so is important for children to learn. It is closely linked to sharing (page 123).

Why children may not take turns

AGE AND STAGE OF DEVELOPMENT

As with sharing, self-regulation is at the heart of turn taking. Children have to control their natural impulse to have something straight away. This level of impulse control is not available for many children until they are three years old.

EXPERIENCE

Some children may not have had much experience of taking turns. It may be that they are the only child and their family members have not required them to take turns. In some cases, children may have learnt to have tantrums or to become aggressive in order to avoid taking turns.

How to respond when children do not take turns

Most of the time, children do not take turns because they are keen to do or have whatever they can see. It is important to pick children up on not taking turns, but at the same time, not make a huge fuss about it. If children are under three years, it is worth moving on but then using preventative strategies to help them learn to take turns. For older children, a simple comment explaining that you have seen that they did not take their turn and then an explanation about how this was unhelpful should suffice.

Turn taking is an important social skill

Helping children to take turns

Children need adults to help them learn to take turns and for this to become a normal behaviour. Turn taking is an important social skill but also supports the development of self-regulation in children. It is worth looking out for various routines within the setting that naturally provide opportunities for turn taking. This might include mealtimes, when children pass food to each other or wait for another child to wash their hands. Playing games with children is another fantastic way of helping them to take turns. Games can start from a very young age. With toddlers, it is possible to take it in turns to create a stack of bricks or to fill up a small bucket with sand. With older children, games such as picture lotto, snap or ludo can be helpful.

ROLE MODELLING

Children can also learn about turn taking if they see adults taking turns, preferably with an explanation, i.e. 'I will just stand and wait until you have finished as you were there first'.

REMINDERS

When an activity or resource is particularly exciting or valued by children, it will be helpful to give children 'at the time' reminders. Some children may also need an adult to wait with them to distract them and also to give encouragement.

PRAISE AND POSITIVE ACKNOWLEDGEMENT

Making sure that children are praised or positively acknowledged will create a culture within a setting where turn taking is clearly a valued skill. It is useful for adults to recognise the action, praise and then explain why it is helpful, e.g. 'Noah, you waited there for Mattie to finish on the slide. That was good turn taking. It meant that no one had an accident'.

Talking to parents

A good starting point is to talk to parents whether they have any issues about turn taking at home. It is useful for parents to understand the importance of turn taking in terms of helping children develop friendships with others, as well as it being a practical social skill. It may be that a child has no siblings, so opportunities to learn about turn taking are limited. If this is the case, it may be that parents might want to adopt some of the strategies that we have looked at to help their child gradually acquire this skill.

Responding to children who are showing several behaviours

It would be unfair to end this book without looking at how we might support children who are showing multiple behaviours. Such children can quickly get a reputation within the setting, and other children and even parents can be quick to pick up on this. The first step when working with such children is to work out the key factors that are affecting their responses. In many cases, there are multiple factors at play, usually including language delay (see page 64). Working constructively with parents to identify these factors and, if appropriate, seek a referral to specialist agencies is important. It can also be useful to do an event chart to see what (if any) triggers there are and also to be aware of how currently adults are responding to the child's behaviour. This can be the starting point for an action plan whereby one or two small aspects of a child's behaviour can be supported.

Ideally, one adult needs to be involved with the child, and this person needs to be genuinely fond of the child and positive about their ability to support the child. This is important because children can sense whether or not someone likes them and also can sense whether or not an adult is confident. Confidence can make children feel secure. Consistency will also be the name of the game as well as looking for opportunities to make the child feel successful. Where older children have a track record of showing inappropriate behaviours, the danger is that they may have not only developed habits about how to respond, but they may also have developed negative feelings about themselves.

Setbacks

One of the features of dealing with children who have more complex needs in terms of behaviour is that it can feel at times as if it is one step forward, two steps back. There are likely to be setbacks, and it is important for the child's later development that these do not prevent adults from continuing to support the child. Parents, in particular, can become disheartened if progress has been made and then a child has a bad day.

Strategies worth considering

These are some of the strategies that I have used with children where several aspects of their behaviour need supporting. No single strategy will work for all children. Often it is a combination of things combined with consistency and patience that can start to make a difference.

SMILES PER HOUR

Set an hourly target for all adults, including parents, to praise or say something positive to the child. Provided that the comments are sincere, it is surprising how quickly this can have an effect on a child. If a reprimand has been given, increase the hourly target for the next couple of hours.

CHANGE THE SCRIPT

Change the script (see page 111) can come into its own with children who have developed habits around their behaviour. Changing the script means anticipating what the child might do and then making sure that the child is not in the situation where they can do this.

RESPONSIBILITY

Some children need opportunities to prove to themselves as well as others that they can show social behaviours. Look for small but meaningful opportunities where children can feel that they are valued, e.g. preparing a snack alongside an adult or being asked for their opinion.

REMINDERS AND VISUAL TIMETABLES

Reminders as well as visual timetables can help children know what they need to do and when to do it. To avoid the child being noticed as 'different', refer the group or other children to the visual timetable as well.

Q

We are working with a child who has multiple difficulties when it comes to behaviour. She is four years old, her language is delayed and her home life is not stable. We have had a few incidents recently when she has lashed out at other children. A couple of the other parents have come to us and asked us not to allow their children to play with her. What should we do?

Your starting point in terms of other parents is to let them know that you have a duty of care towards all children and that no child can be discriminated against. This means that you will protect their child, but you will also ensure that the other child has equal opportunities to access the setting.
In the short term, you will need to be very proactive to prevent this child from harming other children, and you should consider making sure that one adult becomes her play partner in order to keep her busy and supervised. You can also work to increase the amount of interaction that she has while she is in the setting, so that some progress can be made with her language. This has the added benefit of giving her additional adult attention. If you are able to engage with this child's parents, you may like to jointly agree on some consistent strategies that focus on one or two aspects of her behaviour. Finally, you may need to consider whether any aspect of her behaviour is linked with any safeguarding issues at home.

A